9 Steps
TO A GREAT
FEDERAL JOB

9 Steps
TO A GREAT
FEDERAL JOB

Lee Wherry Brainerd
and C Roebuck Reed

LEARNINGEXPRESS ®

NEW YORK

Library of Congress Cataloging-in-Publication Data:
Brainerd, Lee Wherry.
  9 steps to a GREAT federal job / Lee Brainerd, C. Reed.—
    1st ed.
      p. cm.
  ISBN 1-57685-509-0
    1. Civil service positions—United States. 2. Résumés
    (Employment)—United States. I. Title: Nine steps to a
    GREAT federal job. II. Reed, C. Roebuck (Celia
    Roebuck). III. Title.
  JK716.B65 2004
  650.14'2—dc22

                                     2003017068

Printed in the United States of America

9 8 7 6 5 4 3 2 1

First Edition

ISBN 1-57685-509-0

For more information or to place an order, contact LearningExpress at:
  55 Broadway
  8th Floor
  New York, NY 10006

Or visit us at:
  www.learnatest.com

Contents

INTRODUCTION   vii

CHAPTER 1   **TYPES OF FEDERAL JOBS**   1

CHAPTER 2   **HOW TO FIND A FEDERAL JOB**   15

CHAPTER 3   **HOW TO APPLY FOR A FEDERAL JOB**   29

CHAPTER 4   **KSAS AND THE CCAR MODEL**   45

CHAPTER 5   **PREPARING TO WRITE**   53

CHAPTER 6   **CHOOSING THE RIGHT WORDS**   65

CHAPTER 7   **GRAMMAR, SPELLING, MECHANICS, AND USAGE**   85

CHAPTER 8   **FIRST DRAFT TO FINAL DRAFT OF YOUR KSAS**   115

CHAPTER 9   **SAMPLE KSAS AND RESPONSES**   131

Introduction

Is a federal job right for you? Are you a recent high school graduate, unsure of what you want to do, but looking for entry to the work force? Are you about to finish graduate school and ready to put your professional training to good use? Are you an experienced office administrator contemplating a new challenge? Are you an information technology expert who would like to serve your country? Are you a laid-off maintenance mechanic? Are you an executive with experience running a small company who is ready for more job security?

No matter what your educational level, your previous job experience, or your field of interest, there could be a federal job with your name on it! Every year, the U.S. government hires hundreds of thousands of workers to fill existing job vacancies or newly created jobs. Right now there are over 2.7 million federal employees serving this country. In fact, the federal government is the single largest employer in the United States, with workers in every state and in over 200 foreign countries. The average salary of a civil service worker is more than $52,000. Is a federal job sounding better and better?

The reasons citizens elect to pursue civil service are as numerous as the individuals themselves. Often, people are drawn to the fact that the federal government frequently promotes from within, giving preference to employees already within the civil service system. They see government employment as a relatively secure career path, with excellent benefits and an enticing array of possible assignments. Others are looking for summer jobs or temporary work in interesting locations. You have your own good reasons for buying this book and pursuing federal employment.

▶ WHAT WILL THIS BOOK DO FOR ME?

As is the case with any job and any employer, there are more applicants seeking U.S. government employment than there are jobs available. You have wisely started reading this book in order to give yourself an advantage over your fellow applicants. Within these pages, you will find a wealth of information and advice that will help you land the federal job of your dreams.

The U.S. civil service application process is lengthy and complex. In fact, there is not even a single process. Many government agencies have differing sets of procedures for job applicants. However, there is a common thread running through virtually all federal hiring processes. That thread is the KSA.

What Is a KSA?

KSA stands for Knowledge, Skills, and Abilities. Federal hiring laws require all hiring agencies to analyze each job within the agency in order to determine its duties and responsibilities and then to state the knowledge, skills, and abilities required to perform the job effectively. Those statements of necessary qualifications are called KSAs. The statements you must write in response to the agency KSAs are also called KSAs. The two meanings of the term are used interchangeably.

For most federal jobs, you will be asked to write between three and six KSAs. Some complex jobs may require as many as eight. The ability to write effective KSAs is the single most important skill you need to become a successful job applicant. If your KSAs do not demonstrate that you meet the job requirements, it does not matter how much experience you have or how well-suited you are for the position. You will not get the job. You will not even clear the first hurdle toward getting the job.

Intimidated? Don't be. By the time you finish this book, you will be well prepared to write the KSAs that will get you the federal job you want.

What Is In This Book?

There are nine chapters in the book. Step by step the chapters present you with the information you need to research, locate, and secure the federal job that is right for you.

What's In It for Me?

In this book you will learn:

- ▶ major employer agencies and the six categories of federal jobs
- ▶ how to locate federal jobs
- ▶ how to decipher the application process
- ▶ to write KSAs using the CCAR model
- ▶ what to do before you start to write

▶ how to choose exactly the right words
▶ the mechanics of good KSA writing
▶ the KSA writing process
▶ samples and examples of good KSAs

Chapter 1: Types of Federal Jobs

In Chapter 1 you will learn about some of the larger governmental agencies. It may come as no surprise, for example, that the U.S. Postal Service is a major federal employer, but you may be surprised to discover that the U.S. armed forces employ many civilians. In this chapter, you will find out how to get more information about agencies that interest you.

Chapter 1 also explores the six major categories of federal jobs:

▶ student jobs, internships, and temporary positions
▶ trade and labor jobs
▶ professional, administrative, and technical positions
▶ administrative support assistant (clerical jobs)
▶ information technology and telecommunications jobs
▶ senior executive positions

You will learn what general kinds of positions fall within each of these categories, including specific job titles found within each. You will also get a sense of the type of background necessary in each category.

In Chapter 1 you will also learn about the excellent benefits package offered by the federal government to its employees. You will gain insight into federal pay scale plans and learn how to find out what pay level you might expect initially.

Finally, you will read about some of the downsides to federal employment.

Chapter 2: How to Find a Federal Job

In Chapter 2 you will learn how to locate federal job openings. You will be introduced to OPM, the federal Office of Personnel Management, and its website, USAJOBS.opm.gov. This website is the single most important and useful resource for a federal job seeker. You will become familiar with the website, which offers many services for prospective employees.

Highlights of OPM's website include a listing of thousands of currently available jobs. This listing is searchable in several ways, including by area of interest and geographical location. You will learn how to use keywords to conduct a search and how to write and submit your resume online.

Chapter 2 also discusses additional sources for federal job listings. You will learn about telephone job hotlines and federal Employment Service Centers. The chapter discusses other online resources as well as professional recruiters, or headhunters. You will find resources for job listings in print, including magazines and newspapers.

Finally, you will learn how to effectively network to locate job openings within the government. Networking is a practice that will help you start and advance your career in profound and rewarding ways.

Chapter 3: How to Apply for a Federal Job

The first federal job announcement you see may be a shock to you. The typical vacancy listing is long and filled with unfamiliar terminology. In Chapter 3 you can face that shock head-on and get it over with. Once you have gone through the chapter's step-by-step examination of a typical vacancy listing, you will see it is not as hard to understand as it first appeared.

Chapter 3 also shows you how to determine if you are qualified for a particular federal job. The good thing about such a long job announcement is that it tells you in very specific terms what qualifications the listing agency is looking for. You will learn where to look for both the required and the desired qualifications and how to understand quickly whether or not it will be worth your while to apply for the position.

This chapter contains information about how job applications are evaluated and gives you tips about successful application. You will learn about the way education and experience are considered, including how to determine what combinations of the two are qualifying for a particular job.

Many federal jobs require both a short resume and the longer KSAs. Some jobs also require additional application steps. Even though there is no single Civil Service Examination required of all applicants, some positions still require some kind of exam. You will learn what kinds of exams may be required in what kinds of jobs and how to find out more information about them.

Once you know how to read the federal vacancy announcement, you are ready to take the next step, which is to present yourself as the best candidate for your chosen position. The remaining chapters give you detailed instructions for doing just that.

Chapter 4: KSAs and the CCAR Model

Chapter 4 is your introduction to the KSA writing process. KSAs are the heart of your federal job application. They will determine whether or not your application will make it into the pile of qualified applicants, and they will determine your odds of getting a job interview or a job offer.

While KSAs can seem confusing or intimidating at first, you will come to consider them as your allies in securing a federal job. They are concrete evidence that you possess the necessary qualifications for the position you want. If you have ever wondered why you never got called for the job you thought you were perfect for, you will be relieved to know that with federal jobs, there is no mystery.

In this chapter, you will learn the difference between the absolute minimum requirements for a particular job, the Selective Factors, and the optional but desired qualifications, the Quality Ranking Factors. You will also see how to demonstrate, in KSA form, your ability to successfully perform the tasks required in the position.

Think of it this way: a resume reveals little about you. Typically, you have only a few lines to summarize your previous experience. A KSA, on the other hand, gives you the opportunity to talk about your education and experience in terms of details specific to the job for which you are applying.

The model you will follow in writing your KSAs is the CCAR model. CCAR stands for Challenge, Context, Action, Results. Working within the CCAR framework enables you to maximize your education, training, and experience. It also directs you to include the results of your actions. Results are the critical component of KSAs that show potential employers what an effective employee you are.

In Chapter 4, you will learn to follow the CCAR model to write KSAs. You will learn what to include in a KSA and how long each one should be. You will also learn how to identify KSAs even when they are given other names by federal agencies.

Chapter 5: Preparing to Write

As you prepare to write the KSAs that will get you the job you want, it will be to your advantage to spend a lot of time in the prewriting stage. There are a number of specific elements to prewriting, and this chapter covers each one in detail.

You will learn exactly who is reading the KSAs you write. Once you know who reads your KSAs, you can tailor what you write to your audience. For example, KSAs are typically read by at least two separate readers. The first reader determines whether or not you meet the minimum qualifications for the job. Subsequent readers really delve into your responses and rank you against all other job applicants. Typically only the top few applicants get interviews, much less job offers. That is why it is important to know what readers are looking for.

Chapter 5 also helps you define your goal in writing KSAs. Essentially, your goal is to convince the readers that you are the best candidate. You do this by closely aligning your experiences and training to the qualifications of the job you want. You must persuade the reader that you are expert, proficient, and highly qualified or skilled at the Selective Factors and Quality Ranking Factors mentioned in the vacancy announcement.

You will also learn in Chapter 5 how to focus your writing so that your readers understand quickly what it is you want them to know. The readers look at hundreds of applications, and you do not want them to feel you are wasting their time. On the other hand, they are not mind readers, so you must be sure to include all pertinent details about yourself.

Chapter 5 will help you with brainstorming techniques, including the questions to ask yourself before you begin writing. It will teach you how to pick examples from your work and life experiences that showcase your abilities to best advantage. It will also guide you through the outlining process, so that you know what you are going to write before you write it. By the time you finish the chapter, you will be prepared to write KSAs that will get attention and get you the job.

Chapter 6: Choosing the Right Words

There are a number of techniques for choosing the right words, but they all boil down to one principle: You want to use the minimum number of words possible, while achieving maximum impact. That is not a contradiction. Remember that the readers are very busy. You have a limited amount of their time in which to convince them you are the most qualified applicant. Chapter 6 teaches you how to use words wisely, maximize their impact, and minimize their number.

You will learn what kinds of words and expressions to avoid, how to use active voice instead of passive voice, and what kinds of proactive words show you to be the dynamic individual you are. There are useful lists of words to help you do just that.

The chapter discusses the difference between a word's literal meaning—its denotation—and the associations a reader tends to make with the word—its connotation. You will learn how to avoid undesirable connotations and enhance associations favorable to you. Finally, there are guidelines for concise and powerful writing, the kind of writing you must use in preparing successful KSAs.

Chapter 7: Grammar, Spelling, Mechanics, and Usage

Chapter 7 is a review of the basics of good writing. If it has been a while since your last English class, you will welcome this refresher course. Even though you may write on a computer with spell and grammar checkers, these features are far from foolproof. Ultimately, it is up to you to make your prose reflect the best you can do.

Many federal jobs require the ability to communicate in writing. Your KSA response to that requirement must reflect the ability to communicate well in writing. This chapter reminds you of some common pitfalls and prompts your memory on such essentials as the parts of speech, noun/verb agreement, verb tense shifts, and double negatives. It discusses the difference between a proper sentence and a run-on sentence, or a sentence fragment.

There are extensive lists of commonly confused and misused words, complete with correct ways to use them. Once you master these words, you will avoid numerous potential errors in your writing, and the lists are always there for you. As you write, you can refer to the lists to ensure correct usage. There are exercises, as well, to help cement proper usage in your mind.

Chapter 7 ends with a discussion of spelling, business terms, and punctuation. You will find extensive, helpful reference works, including many websites to help you.

Chapter 8: First Draft to Final Draft of Your KSAs

Chapter 8 discusses the actual sitting down and writing, revising, and editing of your KSAs. It guides you as you take the outline you sketched in Chapter 5 and turn it into a final, attention-getting draft.

First you learn about formatting. Formatting gives you the look of your KSA. There are a number of different formats that are acceptable for a KSA. In this chapter you will learn how to select the one that will show you to your best advantage.

After you select a format, you are ready to write. You will be guided as you select details from your brainstorming efforts and match them with the outline you have already written. Then, you will learn how to select the details most relevant to your example and most consistent with the KSA requirement. You will learn how to rework relevant examples to fit similar but different KSAs; and you will learn how to use your KSAs to set yourself above the pack, to make your application stand out. Using leadership language is one way you can distinguish your KSAs from those of your competition, and Chapter 8 includes a discussion of leadership language.

Finally, this chapter reviews effective editing and revision techniques. Revising and editing are the two last steps of writing. Chapter 8 provides specific tips and pointers for revision. These techniques involve taking a first, or rough, draft and tightening and polishing it until it sparkles like the gem you need for it to be. Finally, you will learn the tricks of effective proofreading, to make sure your KSA is error free. When you see the difference between your rough draft and your final draft, you will be glad you took the extra time to polish.

Chapter 9: Sample KSAs and Responses

This chapter contains twenty-four KSA responses to various KSA requirements, reflecting twenty-four jobs listings within the six major categories of federal jobs. The KSAs include examples of many of the common requirements, such as *ability to follow instructions, ability to communicate orally and in writing,* and *ability to plan, manage, and organize projects.* By the time you have studied these sample KSAs, you will be well-equipped to write outstanding KSAs of your own on these and other topics.

▶ GETTING STARTED

If you have read this far, you are ready to embark on the journey that will lead to the right federal job for you. As you have seen, this book will be your trusty companion and guide on this adventure. It is time to get started!

9 Steps

TO A GREAT
FEDERAL JOB

CHAPTER

1

Types of Federal Jobs

Are you considering a government job? You may not know that the federal government is the country's single largest employer, but it is true. This chapter is an introduction to the extraordinary variety of federal jobs. It does not provide an exhaustive list but rather gives an overview of the types of jobs available and a sampling of the federal departments and agencies doing the hiring.

As a result of the government's wide-ranging responsibilities, the types of federal jobs available run the gamut from manual laborer to scientist, from mail carrier to graphic illustrator, from teacher to clerk-typist. There are full-time and part-time jobs, temporary and career positions, jobs that require advanced degrees with extensive experience, and student jobs that are designed to be introductions to the work force. As long as you have a high school diploma or GED and are a U.S. citizen (for most positions) you will meet the requirements for many federal jobs.

There are 15 major departments within the executive branch of the government. It is the executive branch that hires, by far, the most federal workers. In 2001 the executive branch employed 2,645,700 of the 2,710,000 civilians in government service. The largest single employer in the U.S. government, with about 850,000 workers, is the United States Postal Service (USPS). The Department of Defense (DOD) is also a major employer. In 2001 the DOD employed 37% of all civilian federal workers. That percentage translates to 671,600 people working in non-uniformed capacities. In addition to these civilians, the DOD also employs the service men and women in the Armed Forces.

The next largest federal employer is the Department of Veterans Affairs (VA). The VA employs 13% of all civilian workers.

The other departments, which also hire substantial numbers of workers, are:

Department of Agriculture
Department of Commerce
Department of Education
Department of Energy
Department of Health and Human Services
Department of Homeland Security
Department of Housing and Urban Development
Department of Interior
Department of Justice
Department of Labor
Department of State (also referred to as the State Department)
Department of Transportation
Department of the Treasury

▶ A WIDE RANGE OF PROGRAMS

Each of the departments runs a variety of programs related to its central mission. Here is a list of programs run by each of the departments:

▶ **Department of Agriculture**—Farm Service Agency, Foreign Agricultural Service, Food Safety and Inspection Service, Forest Service, Food and Nutrition Service, and Rural Housing Service

▶ **Department of Commerce**—Economic Development Administration, Bureau of the Census, Minority Business Development Agency, National Oceanic and Atmospheric Administration, Patent and Trademark Office, and Office of Technology Policy

▶ **Department of Defense**—Defense Commissary Agency, Defense Contract Audit Agency, Defense Intelligence Agency, National Imagery and Mapping Agency, and the National Security Agency/Central Security Service

▶ **Department of Education**—Bilingual Education and Minority Languages Affairs, Civil Rights, Institute of Education Sciences, Special Education and Rehabilitative Services, Student Financial Assistance Programs, and Vocational and Adult Education

▶ **Department of Energy**—Energy Efficiency and Renewable Energy; Energy Information; Environment, Safety and Health; Office of Science; Federal Energy Regulatory Commission, and National Nuclear Security Administration

▶ **Department of Health and Human Services**—Administration for Children and Families, Centers for Disease Control and Prevention, Food and Drug Administration, National Institutes of Health, and Substance Abuse and Mental Health Services Administration

- ▶ **Department of Homeland Security**—Bureau of Customs and Border Protection, Bureau of Immigration and Customs Enforcement, Transportation Security Administration, Federal Emergency Management Agency, National Communications System, and Office of Emergency Preparedness
- ▶ **Department of Housing and Urban Development**—Community Planning and Development, Government National Mortgage Association, Office of Fair Housing and Equal Opportunity, and Office of Healthy Homes and Lead Hazard Control
- ▶ **Department of Interior**—Bureau of Indian Affairs; Bureau of Land Management; Fish and Wildlife Service; Geological Survey; National Interagency Fire Center; National Park Service; and Office of Surface Mining, Reclamation and Enforcement
- ▶ **Department of Justice**—Alcohol, Tobacco, Firearms and Explosives; Drug Enforcement Agency; Federal Bureau of Investigation; Federal Bureau of Prisons; Foreign Claims Settlement Commission; and U.S. Marshals Service
- ▶ **Department of Labor**—Bureau of International Labor Affairs; Bureau of Labor Statistics; Employment and Training Administration; Office of Disability Employment Policy; Occupational Safety and Health Administration; and Women's Bureau
- ▶ **Department of State**—Arms Control and International Security; Economic, Business, and Agricultural Affairs; Global Affairs; Political Affairs; Public Diplomacy and Public Affairs; and U.S. Mission to the United Nations
- ▶ **Department of Transportation**—Bureau of Transportation Statistics, Federal Aviation Administration, Federal Highway Administration, Maritime Administration, National Highway Traffic Safety Administration, and Research and Special Programs Administration
- ▶ **Department of the Treasury**—Alcohol and Tobacco Tax and Trade Bureau, Bureau of Engraving and Printing, Financial Management Service, Internal Revenue Service, Office of Enforcement, U.S. Secret Service, and U.S. Mint
- ▶ **Department of Veterans Affairs**—Veterans Health Administration, Veterans Benefits Administration, and National Cemetery Administration

Independent Agencies

In addition to the previous departments, there are also a number of independent agencies within the federal government. Some of those agencies employ thousands of workers. Here are some of the larger agencies:

- ▶ Environmental Protection Agency (EPA)
- ▶ General Services Administration (GSA)
- ▶ National Aeronautics and Space Administration (NASA)
- ▶ Small Business Administration (SBA)
- ▶ Social Security Administration (SSA)
- ▶ Equal Employment Opportunity Commission (EEOC)
- ▶ Federal Communications Commission (FCC)
- ▶ Federal Deposit Insurance Commission (FDIC)
- ▶ National Labor Relations Board (NLRB)
- ▶ Agency for International Development (AID)

HELPFUL HINT—CHECK JOB TITLES

Remember that every agency has many types of jobs. For example, if you are not interested in being a soldier, you might not bother checking job listings for the Army. The Army, however, actually employs civilian computer engineers, health technicians, and firefighters, not to mention painters, electricians, and police officers, among many others. Don't let the name fool you!

A Job for You

No matter what your interests are, no matter what your educational background or work experience is, there are federal jobs that will appeal to you and for which you are qualified. Remember, the U.S. government employs millions of people.

When looking for federal jobs, your more pressing problem is how to narrow the search to jobs you are interested in and qualified for. Fortunately, the government has made it fairly easy to find the jobs that are right for you.

In Chapter 2, you will learn how to effectively search for federal jobs. First, however, you need to understand the major categories of government jobs and the classification system used by the Office of Personnel Management (OPM).

▶ THE SIX CATEGORIES OF FEDERAL JOBS

There are six major categories of federal jobs. Here is some general information about each category. Later in this section, you will find information about specific job titles available within each category.

1. **Student/Internships/Temporary.** The Student Educational Employment Program is designed to provide jobs for those who are not at this time looking for permanent career opportunities. It offers a wide range of positions for anyone who is currently enrolled at least half time in an educational program leading to a degree.

    In the Student Temporary Employment component of the program, student employees typically work for several months or years while they are completing their education. Often these are summer jobs or part-time positions during the school year. Even high school students are eligible for this program, as long as they meet the age requirements for work. The work is not necessarily related to the student's course of study, and it tends to pay at least as well as comparable work in the private sector.

    The Student Career Experience component is designed to provide meaningful experience which will further the student's career goals. Positions within this component are similar to internships in that they require coordination between the student's school and the employing governmental agency. These jobs are highly competitive, but they offer excellent experience and opportunities to network within the agency. From some positions a student can move upon graduation into permanent, full-time work without going through the application process. At that point there is a requirement that the prospective employee be a U.S. citizen.

GRADUATE-LEVEL OPPORTUNITIES

There are also two types of internships designed for university graduates. The Presidential Management Internship Program attracts those whose interest lies in public policy analysis and management. They are recruited by every cabinet department and by many independent agencies as future leaders and policy makers. This program requires a graduate degree for eligibility, and there is a nominating process. The Federal Career Intern Program is designed for college graduates without advanced degrees and does not require nomination. It is a two-year appointment that can lead to an offer of permanent employment in any of a wide range of fields.

2. **Trades and Labor.** Those who already know or want to learn a trade or to perform manual labor have lots of options within the federal government. Almost every department or agency lists job openings for vocational workers. In most situations there is much opportunity for advancement.

3. **Professional, Administrative, and Technical Positions.** Many federal employees fall into this category. Every agency and departmental program needs administrative workers. Most hire a variety of professionals with degrees in a wide range of fields. Technical workers with education and/or experience are also in demand in many agencies.

4. **Administrative Support Assistant (Clerical).** Clerical workers go by many job titles in the federal government, as in the private sector. And, as in private enterprise, they are a category of workers no department can function without. There are job opportunities for administrative support workers in every governmental agency.

5. **Information Technology and Telecommunications.** These jobs are expanding in number and variety as rapidly as the technology itself. Increasingly, governmental agencies value those who are trained and/or experienced in this field of work.

6. **Senior Executive.** Senior executives may work their way up through the ranks of government service or they may enter the federal workforce after years in the private sector. Agencies are given considerable hiring latitude in an effort to ensure that the most highly qualified leaders have the opportunity to hold these senior positions.

Student/Internships/Temporary Positions

Many of the student jobs you will find in the federal government are temporary summer jobs. Some jobs are designed to last a year or more on a part-time basis, while student workers attend school. There are also internships, which may very well lead to permanent career positions in the government.

Temporary jobs can be classified as **outdoor jobs**, **clerical jobs**, and **other positions**. Many of the outdoor jobs are with the National Parks Service and the Forest Service.

This is a sampling of commonly available **outdoor jobs**:

- ▶ Animal Packer (cares for and works with pack animals)
- ▶ Biological Technician (plant and wildlife) (assists biological and zoological scientists)
- ▶ Engineering Equipment Operator
- ▶ Forestry Technician (fire)
- ▶ Laborer (trails)
- ▶ Motor Vehicle Operator
- ▶ Physical Sciences Technician (non-professional work in the fields of astronomy, chemistry, geology, geophysics, health physics, hydrology, metallurgy, oceanography, physics, and other physical sciences)
- ▶ Recreation Aid (lifeguard)
- ▶ Survey Aid and Technician

These jobs are **clerical** in nature:

- ▶ Clerk (temporary clerical and administrative support positions; i.e., cash clerk, communications technician, office clerk, visitor use assistant, etc.)
- ▶ Information Receptionist
- ▶ Research Clerks/Assistants

These types of student jobs are **neither clerical nor outdoors**:

- ▶ Food Service Worker
- ▶ Laundry Worker
- ▶ Mail Clerk
- ▶ Child Care Worker
- ▶ Materials Handler (Warehouse)
- ▶ Legal Clerk

The student intern may work for any of a number of agencies, and duties will vary accordingly. The work may be technical or administrative in nature or complex, depending on the grade of the position. (The position grading system will be discussed at the end of this chapter.) The intern's work will offer experience that is related to the academic field of study. If you are interested in pursuing an internship, you may find it helpful to look through the types of jobs listed under *Professional, Administrative, and Technical Positions* later in this chapter, remembering that these are merely representative of the types of jobs available, not an exhaustive list.

HELPFUL HINT—ASK THE EXPERTS

If you are a student and you are interested in an internship with the federal government, check with your school's career counseling or career placement office. They can help you with information and guidance about opportunities, deadlines, and the application process.

Trades and Labor Positions

There is tremendous variety within this category, often referred to as blue-collar or manual labor. The variation extends to both the nature of the work performed and the extent of responsibility required of the worker, with the pay range reflecting this variety.

Here is a list of some of the broad areas of employment for those interested in the trades and labor. Many of the areas have several levels of positions, from apprentice/assistant to supervisor.

Able-Bodied Seaman	Industrial Equipment Operator
Air Conditioning Equipment Mechanic	Laborer
Animal Caretaker	Laundry Worker
Audio-Visual Operator	Lineman
Automotive Mechanic	Maintenance Mechanic
Cemetery Caretaker	Maintenance Worker
Cook	Mason
Custodial Worker	Motor Vehicle Operator
Electrician	Sewing Machine Operator
Engineering Equipment Operator	Tractor Operator
Fisherman	Tree Worker
Food Service Worker	Warehouse Worker
Gardener	Water Treatment Plant Operator
Housekeeping Aid	

Professional, Administrative, and Technical Positions

There is scarcely a professional or technical field that is not represented in the federal government. Of course, all those professionals and technicians (not to mention the students, laborers, and technicians) need administrators to keep things running smoothly.

This is a small sampling of the kinds of positions available in multiple agencies for professionals, administrators, and technical workers:

Agricultural Commodity Grader
Agricultural Extension Specialist
Air Safety Investigator
Air Traffic Controller
Animal Health Technician
Appraiser
Archeologist
Architect
Archives Technician
Attorney
Audiovisual Production Specialist
Bank Examiner
Benefits Specialist, Federal Retirement
Biological Science Technician
Biologist
Bond Sales Promotion Specialist
Border Patrol Agent
Botanist
Canine Enforcement Officer
Cemetery Administrator
Chemical Engineer
Chemist
Claims Examiner
Clerk of the Court
Clothing Designer
Commissary Store Manager
Community Planner
Copyright Specialist
Copyright Technician
Correctional Institution Administrator
County Executive Director
Crop Insurance Administrator
Cryptographer
Customs Entry and Liquidation Officer
Dental Assistant
Dietitian
Economics Assistant (technician)

Educator (including Rehabilitation Specialist, Teacher, Administrator, and Training Instructor)
Engineer, Agricultural
Engineer, Chemical
Engineer, Fire Protection
Engineer, Safety
Engineering Drafting Technician
Equipment Manager
Estate Tax Examiner
Facilities Manager
Financial Administration and Program Manager
Fingerprint Identification Specialist (technician)
Foreign Law Specialist
Geneticist
Geographer
Health Insurance Administrator
Health System Administrator
Historian
Human Resources Worker (including Employee Relations Specialist, Labor Relations Specialist, Mediator, and Position Classification Specialist)
Inspector, Food
Intelligence Specialist
Internal Revenue Officer
International Relations Specialist
Laundry and Dry Cleaning Plant Manager
Law Clerk
Legal Instruments Examiner (technician)
Library Technician
Loan Specialist
Logistics Manager
Management Analyst

Management and Program Assistant
  (technician)
Marshal, Deputy
Mathematical Statistician
Medical Records Administrator
Medical Records Technician
Microbiologist
Museum Curator
Nuclear Medicine Technician
Nurse
Park Ranger
Passport Examiner
Pathology Technician
Pharmacist
Photographer
Police Officer

Program Analyst
Psychologist
Realty Specialist
Security Administrator
Social Insurance Administrator
Social Worker
Supply Clerical and Technician
Supply Program Manager
Support Services Manager
Surveying Technician
Therapist, Physical
Therapist, Recreation
Underwriter, Crop Insurance
Unemployment Insurance Specialist
Veterinary Medical Scientist
Writer, Technical

Administrative Support Assistant (Clerical) Positions

No public or private enterprise can carry on its business without the support of clerks and assistants. The federal government employs thousands of clerical workers. These are some of the job titles available.

Agricultural Commodity Aid
Air Traffic AssistantBudget Clerk and
  Assistant
Cash Processing ClerkClerk and Assistant
Clerk Stenographer and ReporterClerk-
  Typist
Coding ClerkCommunications Equipment
  Operator
Communications Clerk
Computer Clerk and Assistant
Correspondence ClerkData Transcriber
Editorial AssistantEqual Opportunity Assis-
  tant
Equipment OperatorFinancial Clerk and
  Technician
Federal Clerical Worker

Human Resources AssistantIntelligence Aid
  and Clerk
Language ClerkLegal Assistant
Mail and File ClerkManagement and Pro-
  gram Clerk and Assistant
Medical Support Assistant
MessengerOffice Automation Clerk and
  Assistant
Printing Clerical
Receptionist Sales Store Clerk
SecretarySecurity Clerk and Assistant
Social Services Aid and AssistantStatistical
  Assistant
Telephone OperatorTransportation Clerk
  and Assistant

Information Technology and Telecommunications Positions

Information Technology (IT) is a rapidly growing field, with knowledgeable workers often in demand. The federal government includes telecommunications jobs in the same general category. Both areas deal with rapidly evolving systems. Here is a representative sampling of positions.

Applications Software Developer	Customer Support
Automation Specialist	Information Technology Specialist
Biologist (Data Manager)	Network Systems Specialist
Computer Assistant	Operating Systems Specialist
Computer Engineer	Patent Examiner (computer-related fields)
Computer Operations	Policy and Planning
Computer Operator	Systems Administration
Computer Scientist	Systems Analyst
Computer Specialist	Telecommunications Specialist

Senior Executive Positions

Senior Executives are much in demand in the federal government. They are the leaders and the policy makers. Government agencies promote from within, and they also search for seasoned executives from the private sector. Every agency and all of the programs of those agencies need Senior Executives. These are the kinds of positions filled by such workers.

Administrative Judges	Deputy Assistant Directors
Administrators	Deputy Directors
Assistant Administrators	Directors
Associate Chief Financial Officers	Executive Directors
Associate Directors	General Counsels
Chief Financial Officers (CFO)	Managers
Chief Officers	Senior Advisors
Chief Scientific and Technical Advisors	Senior Research Scientists

The Rewards of Government Service

There are many reasons to go to work for the U.S. Government. Some of them are tangible: The benefits package and pay are required by law to be comparable to private sector employment. There is room for advancement, both in pay and in responsibility. And there are well-established avenues for conflict resolution and airing grievances.

There are also intangible rewards for government employment: The opportunity to serve your country in an important and meaningful way is a powerful incentive for many citizens. It doesn't hurt that federal careers tend to be more secure than many in private industry. And the sheer variety of government jobs means that there are extensive opportunities for both advancement and career change. Do you like to travel? The federal government posts employees to every state and territory and to most foreign countries. Need an unconventional work schedule? Many governmental agencies offer flexible schedules, telecommuting, and part-time work.

Benefits

In an era of shrinking and endangered benefits packages in the workplace, the federal government stands out as a generous employer. **Benefits** is a term applied to a collection of extras which may or may not be offered by an employer. Those extras include health insurance, sick leave, vacations and holidays, and retirement plans.

Health and Life Insurance

The government offers a variety of health plans to its employees and their families. As is the situation with many private sector jobs, the worker pays a share of the health plan cost and the government pays a larger share. No matter what department or agency you work for, the health benefits are attractive; and they are comparable among agencies and in different locales. Workers may choose among HMOs and fee-for-service plans, as they are available in a given geographical area. Federal employees are also covered by disability insurance.

The optional Federal Employees' Group Life Insurance (FEGLI) Program is the largest group life insurance program in the world. It covers over four million federal employees and retirees and many of their family members. The government pays a third of the cost of the term life insurance coverage for those employees who elect to participate in the program.

Federal Holidays

There are ten federal holidays, and virtually every civilian federal employee gets them. Very few private firms offer all of these. Here are the federal holidays.

New Year's Day	Labor Day
Martin Luther King, Jr's Birthday	Columbus Day
President's Day	Veterans Day
Memorial Day	Thanksgiving Day
Independence Day	Christmas Day

Leave Policies

The federal government is generous with regard to annual leave (vacation), sick leave, and family and medical leave policies. Annual leave is awarded based on the employee's length of service; the longer the time on the job, the more vacation days. The range is 13 to 26 days per year. Even part-time employees accrue vacation leave.

Sick leave is 13 days a year, with no limit to the number of days that can be accrued. An employee may use sick leave for personal medical needs, to care for a family member, even for adoption-related purposes.

The federal government also offers up to twelve weeks of unpaid leave during any twelve-month period under the Family and Medical Leave Act. If the employee becomes a parent or the employee or a family member has serious health conditions, the worker may take the necessary time off and be guaranteed a return to the same job with no penalty.

Retirement

The Civil Service Retirement System (CSRS) covers federal workers who meet the minimum requirements for age and length of service. Retired workers are also eligible to continue their health coverage. And the CSRS is as secure as a retirement plan can be, which can be reassuring in times of uncertainty.

The federal government also offers the Thrift Savings Plan, which is similar to a 401(k) plan for those who elect to participate. In addition, the Social Security system covers federal employees.

The Flip Side

You have taken a look at the benefits of working for the federal government. Now take a moment to examine the other side of the coin. There are potential downsides to federal employment as well as benefits.

Many of the drawbacks come from the fact that the government is the single largest employer in the country. Like many large organizations, it is more sluggish than responsive when a change needs to be made. There are often many layers of approvals required for any action that is not routine. Things tend to move slowly in the civil service; if you are the impatient type, this could be a problem for you.

Because of the job security, there are many federal employees who know their jobs are safe no matter how mediocre their performance may be. That takes away a common incentive to work hard. Some of these people feel a need to excel because of personal pride or a desire to serve others; some do not, and there is not much to be done about that. If your co-workers fall into the latter group, you may have to pick up some of the slack created by their lack of motivation.

Finally, at the upper levels of career employment government pay does not always keep pace with remuneration in private enterprise. Top professionals and administrators in the federal work force seldom make what their counterparts in industry do. You have to decide whether or not the trade-offs in terms of job security, benefits, and service to country are worth the lower pay ceiling.

The Pay Dirt

There are two main systems of pay classification within the federal government: the General Schedule (GS) system and the Wage System (WS). Almost 75% of all federal workers are paid under the GS system, about 12% are WS workers, and the rest are covered under other pay systems. Postal Service employees, for example, are compensated under a separate USPS pay system. In the USPS system, base pay, overtime, and night and Sunday pay are designed to be comparable to private industry pay.

The Wage System covers federal employees who are paid by the hour. The aim of the Wage System, like the USPS system, is to provide equitable wages between government and private workers. The government works with labor organizations to ensure that WS employees are paid comparably to other trade and labor workers who perform similar jobs in their local wage area.

Because hourly wages vary by geographic location, a WS Air Conditioning Mechanic, for example, in one locale will earn somewhat more (or less) than one performing the same job in a different locale. The buying power of the different hourly wages tends to be similar, however; as higher local wages are often a result of a higher local cost of living.

There are 15 pay grades for non-supervisory wageworkers. Each grade has five steps, allowing for raises in pay, comparable to those in private industry. Supervisory workers have their own wage schedules, based on the WS non-supervisory schedules.

The General Schedule system is designed to cover salaried workers. These are often called white-collar workers, and they make up most of the federal work force. Each worker's job is given a GS number from one to fifteen, depending on its determined value, with one being the bottom rung of the pay ladder. Within each GS number, there are ten steps to allow for pay raises without a promotion in grade. The pay for a GS-1 worker, for example, ranges between $15,214 (step one) and $19,031 (step ten).

SALARY TABLE 2003-GS
INCORPORATING A 3.10% GENERAL INCREASE
EFFECTIVE JANUARY 2003
ANNUAL RATES BY GRADE AND STEP

Grade	Step 1	Step 2	Step 3	Step 4	Step 5	Step 6	Step 7	Step 8	Step 9	Step 10	Within-Grade Amounts
GS-1	$15,214	$15,722	$16,228	$16,731	$17,238	$17,536	$18,034	$18,538	$18,559	$19,031	VARIES
GS-2	17,106	17,512	18,079	18,559	18,767	19,319	19,871	20,423	20,975	21,527	VARIES
GS-3	18,664	19,286	19,908	20,530	21,152	21,774	22,396	23,018	23,640	24,262	622
GS-4	20,952	21,650	22,348	23,046	23,744	24,442	25,140	25,838	26,536	27,234	698
GS-5	23,442	24,223	25,004	25,785	26,566	27,347	28,128	28,909	29,690	30,471	781
GS-6	26,130	27,001	27,872	28,743	29,614	30,485	31,356	32,227	33,098	33,969	871
GS-7	29,037	30,005	30,973	31,941	32,909	33,877	34,845	35,813	36,781	37,749	968
GS-8	32,158	33,230	34,302	35,374	36,446	37,518	38,590	39,662	40,734	41,806	1,072
GS-9	35,519	36,703	37,887	39,071	40,255	41,439	42,623	43,807	44,991	46,175	1,184
GS-10	39,115	40,419	41,723	43,027	44,331	45,635	46,939	48,243	49,547	50,851	1,304
GS-11	42,976	44,409	45,842	47,275	48,708	50,141	51,574	53,007	54,440	55,873	1,433
GS-12	51,508	53,225	54,942	56,659	58,376	60,093	61,810	63,527	65,244	66,961	1,717
GS-13	61,251	63,293	65,335	67,377	69,419	71,461	73,503	75,545	77,587	79,629	2,042
GS-14	72,381	74,794	77,207	79,620	82,033	84,446	86,859	89,272	91,685	94,098	2,413
GS-15	85,140	87,978	90,816	93,654	96,492	99,330	102,168	105,006	107,844	110,682	2,838

Source: www.opm.gov/oca/03tables/pdf/gs.pdf

It has been the practice of the federal government to offer cost of living adjustments to the GS and WS pay scales. That means you may anticipate regular raises in pay without achieving a promotion in grade or responsibility.

The GS system also offers pay adjustments based on geographic location. This is implemented by means of a base scale, with pay adjustments for local areas with a higher cost of living. As of 2003, geographical pay adjustments range from 9.62% to 21.08% above base pay in the continental United States and may be even higher outside the contiguous states. In addition, there may be a pay adjustment for work performed in a remote area or under undesirable working conditions.

For example, a GS-1 worker, starting at Step One with no adjustment would earn $15,214 annually. That same worker in Atlanta, however, would receive a geographical adjustment of 10.85%, for a starting salary of $16,865. A GS-1 Step One worker in Seattle would start at $17,209 (a 13.11% adjustment); in Boston, $17,496 (15%); and in San Francisco, $18,421 (21.08%). Government employees in San Francisco and the Bay Area surrounding it receive the highest geographical pay adjustment in the continental United States. For a complete set of tables showing pay adjustments, go to www.opm.gov/oca/03tables/pdf/03saltbl.pdf.

As you may realize by reading the salary table, GS levels one and two are entry-level positions. Often, no more than a high school diploma or GED is needed to secure one of these jobs. A GS level three or four position normally requires some higher education, whether college or business or technical school. At GS levels five through seven, an applicant must usually have a college degree or substantial work experience, or a combination of the two that satisfies the work/education requirements of the job. A GS-8 through GS-12 position entails considerably more responsibility, and a successful applicant will need either a college or postgraduate degree or a substantial amount of experience in a relevant field, or both. A GS-13 through GS-15 position requires either a top-level, highly specialized educational background or management experience, or both.

▶ SUMMARY

No matter what your interests, and regardless of your educational background and prior work experience, there is a federal job that could suit you. It can be intimidating and frustrating, however, to find out about the right positions and even more challenging to go through the application process and actually land the right job. The next two chapters will show you how to locate the jobs you are interested in and how to successfully negotiate the application process.

2

How to Find a Federal Job

Now you know what kinds of opportunities the federal government offers. You may be wondering how to find out what is available now, what jobs are actually open at any given moment. This chapter will tell you how to find the open positions, and how you can take your first step toward civil service employment.

The United States Office of Personnel Management (OPM) is the federal government's official source for federal job listings. Listings of current job openings can be accessed either online or via telephone. It can be daunting to find your way through the massive listings to locate the jobs you are interested in, but the good news is that the listings can be searched in a variety of ways. The logic of the listings, and how to find them, will follow.

All About USAJOBS

The most comprehensive Internet listing of open federal positions is on www.usajobs.opm.gov. If you go to www.usajobs.opm.gov, you will find information on job vacancies all over the world. The information is updated daily, and it is drawn from OPM's database of more than 17,000 job opportunities. Best of all, there is no fee for using the USAJOBS website. The homepage of this site has several features, including Featured Job and Featured Employer, a schedule of Job Fairs and other events, Jobs in Demand, and e-scholar, which has information on programs for students, such as internships. These links highlight different jobs, employers, and jobs in high demand for a short time. When you go to

HELPFUL HINT—GET ONLINE

The Internet makes it relatively easy to search for a government job. Using the Internet is convenient, if you have access to a computer. If you don't have your own computer, most schools and public libraries now provide Internet access. Private establishments, such as cyber cafes, also offer connection to the World Wide Web. Information is available on the Internet 24 hours a day, seven days a week.

the site, these might catch your eye, and clicking on them will provide you with a detailed snapshot of these topics.

However, if you really need extra help finding a federal job that is right for you, this site has a feature called the Career Interests Center. You can look for jobs based on your interests (Career Interest Guide), you can look for jobs with duties you enjoy (Job Interest Matching), you can research the details of a specific job (Specific Job Exploration), or if you are currently working in the private sector, you can find a corresponding federal job (Match Federal Jobs to Private Sector Jobs).

When you are ready to get started, click on *Search Jobs*.

JOBS IN DEMAND

Jobs In Demand, features hard-to-fill positions. Jobs are usually posted for two to three weeks in this special section. If you see the job for you in this section, you will know that your skills and interests are in demand.

▶ SEARCH JOBS

Now you know where to start. As the name implies, the *Search Jobs* button will allow you to search jobs. When you first click on this button, you may be feeling overwhelmed by the sheer quantity of available information; you may be wondering how you will ever find the job you are looking for. The best strategy for finding your special job is to start with what you know you want. Fortunately, USAJOBS gives you several options to refine your search, including keyword, location, occupational series, and agency.

Search by Keyword

The first search option you have is to search by keyword. For instance, if you know that you want a position as a driver, you can type the word *driver* into the search box; and all listings that contain that word will be selected for you to see. You could also type in *aircraft*, or *teacher*, or *forest*, or any other word you can think of to describe a type of job that would interest you. In that way you can explore the range of jobs offered within your areas of interest. Do not depend on this method exclusively, however. A similar job that does not contain that particular keyword will not be found with a keyword search. If you type in *airplane* rather than *aircraft*, for example, you might get fewer jobs in your search results.

Search by Location

Do you want to limit your search to a particular geographic area? Most federal job search engines, including the USAJOBS website, allow you to limit your search to jobs in a particular city or state or a single overseas location. This is especially helpful if you do not want to relocate, or if you are looking for a position somewhere new. A search of all the jobs in a particular location will give you a good idea of the agencies that hire in that area as well as the kinds of positions that are available.

Search by Series Number

One of the most useful ways to search for jobs on the OPM website is to search by series number. Federal occupations are grouped into over 500 Occupational Series, and each one is given a four-digit numerical code for identification. To start this search, click on the Occupational Series that interests you in the "Occupational Series" box.

Each occupational series is part of an Occupational Group. You can find the Occupational Group in the first two numbers of the numerical code. For example, if you are interested in a job in education, you will want to enter the number 17 into the "Series Number Search" box. All jobs in education will then come up in your search. If you know that you want to apply for an Education Research Analyst position, you can either click on that series title in the Occupational Series box or enter the number for an Education Research Analyst (1730) in the Series Number Search box.

The results of your Occupational Series or Occupational Group search will be displayed on a Job Summaries page. Each summary lists the opening date for the job (when it was first listed), who may apply, the pay plan (GS or WS level), the appointment term (permanent or temporary), the closing date, the salary, the agency, and the location of the job. Clicking on the job title takes you to the job announcement, where you will find detailed information, such as qualifications and duties.

Applicant Eligibility

During your job search, you can include your eligibility in your search. For example, if you are already a current federal employee in a competitive position, you will be eligible for a wider variety of jobs. You should answer the eligibility question honestly. It will not help you to see jobs for which you are not eligible.

Advanced Searching

As you conduct your search, you can use any combination of the search options you wish. If you are just starting out, you might want to start with keywords and locations. The more you know about the job you are looking for, the more specific you can make your search.

On any of the Search Jobs pages, you will see a list of "Search by" options on the right side. If you click on "Advanced," you will be taken to a page that helps you use any combination of keywords, location, salary, and agency to help you refine your search. The box at the top of the "Advanced Search" page is a "Keyword Search" box. Under this box is underlined text that says "More Tips." Clicking on this phrase will take you to a page of tips for effectively using each part of the "Advanced Search" page.

Also, this website gives you two options for how you want the results of your search to appear. You can sort your results by date (the date the job is posted) or by keyword relevance (how closely the job matches the keyword(s) you enter). You also have the option of seeing a brief description of the job listing, or you can view a detailed description.

STUDENT JOBS

Students looking for jobs with the federal government have an even more direct way to search. Interested students can go directly to www.studentjobs.gov. Students will find the same search engine found on the other site.

Your Agency of Choice

Perhaps you want to work for a particular governmental agency. If so, you can go directly to the website of specific agencies. For example, if you are interested in the Administration for Children and Families, you can go directly to their website and click on Jobs. If you don't know the website of the agency that interests you, or if you want to see a complete list of agencies, use the "Government Links" section found on www.usajobs.opm.gov, or by going through the central federal website www.firstgov.gov. You may find more listings on the agency site, since it is more directly connected to employment in that department than USAJOBS.

EXCEPTED SERVICE AGENCIES

Some federal agencies, such as the FBI and the USPS, are Excepted Service agencies. That means they are not part of the Competitive Civil Service system and have their own hiring systems and procedures. Positions with these agencies can be located by contacting the agencies directly, either by phone or online.

▶ CREATE A RESUME

From the USAJOBS homepage (www.usajobs.opm.gov), your other option aside from searching jobs is creating a resume. MyUSAJOBS is a service that allows you to post your resume for potential employers, apply to jobs online, and receive notification when a job you are interested in becomes available.

You must register for MyUSAJOBS, however it is a free service. Once you have created a username and password, finding and applying for a federal job gets much easier.

Build Your Resume Online

The USAJOBS site also offers a resume building service. In some cases, you can find out about an opening, customize your resume online, and apply without ever leaving your computer. If you prefer, you can print the resume and mail it to the appropriate agency.

▶ JOB POSTINGS

Once you have narrowed your search and you have found a job or jobs that interest you, you can learn everything you need to know from the job listing. Each listing is linked to the job announcement posted by the hiring agency. U.S. government job postings are sometimes difficult to decipher. They will be discussed in detail in Chapter 3, but each announcement will include information such as the salary range for the position, the duties involved, and minimum requirements for the job. Often interested job seekers can apply immediately to the posting agency, using the USAJOBS resume submission process.

If you find yourself intimidated by all the information you read, you might want to start with the Frequently Asked Questions (FAQs). There are also instructions on the website that can clarify any questions you still may have. Take the time to really look around on the USAJOBS site. The better you understand the services OPM offers, the more success you will have finding the right federal job for you.

▶ OTHER ONLINE OPTIONS

There are a number of companies with Internet sites. One website, www.jobsearch.org, is not government-run but is affiliated with several government agencies, including the Department of Defense, the Department of Commerce, and the OPM itself. Your state government's website will also have job listings online.

Buyer Beware

If you prefer the services of a for-profit federal job search engine, go to www.fedjobs.com. This site has free job listings but also sells memberships and books. However, one caution worth heeding is that a number of companies, both on the Internet and by mail order, will try to sell you information on federal jobs that is readily available for free from government sources. The U.S. government itself has issued a warning on the subject, and is following up with prosecutions of some of the most blatant offenders.

The OPM calls these companies scam artists, noting that they often place ads in newspapers and periodicals offering to help job seekers find and secure federal jobs. The companies often try to make themselves sound official, using "U.S." or "Federal" in their company names. They may refer to hidden jobs or listings and imply that only they have access to them, or they may make guarantees of employment or high test scores. The OPM and the Federal Trade Commission warn you to beware of these practices.

▶ RESOURCES IN PRINT

Government Publications

Although the Internet can make the volume of federal jobs more manageable, there are other ways to access the same information, particularly if you know what kind of job you are interested in. The OPM publishes guides to the various occupational families, and those publications are available in many libraries as well as in local OPM Employment Service Centers (ESC) and federal agency personnel offices. The *Qualification Standards Operating Manual*, the *Handbook of Occupational Groups and Series* and the *Position Classification Standards* are three of the most comprehensive and basic publications about the job families. Also, as you would if you were researching online, you may want to start by learning more about the various federal agencies as well as the kinds of job openings each agency might have.

If you are researching government publications, you might want to look at the U.S. Department of Labor, Bureau of Labor Statistics' publication *The Occupational Outlook Quarterly*. This periodical can give you a good idea of national employment trends.

Use the Library

As you start to close in on the agencies and occupations you are interested in, your local reference librarian can help you access other print resources, including microfiche documents, which will be useful in your search. Remember also to ask the librarian about any professional publications in your areas of interest.

HELPFUL HINT—JOBS AWARDED BY APPOINTMENT

Top executives, as well as their advisors and support personnel, may be chosen by noncompetitive appointment. To find out about these positions, use the FederaLIST, which lists over 8,000 federal civil service leadership and support positions. This information is also published in The United States Government Policy and Supporting Positions (usually called the "Plum Book").

Check the Paper

The local newspaper, which used to be the best source for job openings, is experiencing serious competition from the Internet. However, as a job seeker, you can leave no avenue unexplored in your quest for work. If you don't subscribe to your local paper, you can look through the classified job listings at the library. Many newspapers are also online now. Sunday is the best day to check for new listings, and it is important to check frequently.

▶ USE THE PHONE

Job Hotlines

Remember that there are federal job openings not listed with OPM and never placed in the newspaper. Some of the best jobs, in fact, are open for such a brief time that even a day's delay on your part could mean you never find out about them at all. One way to stay current on job openings is to use job hotlines.

There are thousands of job **hotlines** throughout the United States. You will find an excellent directory of job hotlines in a book called *National Job Hotline Directory*, by Sue Cubbage and Marcia Williams. The 6,500 hotline numbers are listed state-by-state, and then alphabetically by company. The directory lists federal government hotlines, as well as other types of hotlines.

The central federal hotline is a voice-response system at 478-757-3000 (TDD 478-744-2299). The automated system will guide you through job vacancy listings, information on the application process, and even some applications for jobs over the phone. This is not a toll-free call, so be prepared by doing as much research as possible before you call. The hotline is also available around-the-clock. You can call at night and on weekends, when phone rates are cheaper.

When you call a job hotline, have a pen and paper with you. Usually these hotlines list recorded information about the jobs available, so you will need to take careful notes. If it is possible, find out when the hotlines are updated so that you don't waste time calling to hear the same information twice.

Contact Government Agencies

Your local telephone directory will have pages in the front of the book that list government agencies. In larger cities these listings will include federal agencies. Call these agencies directly and ask to speak with the human resources department. Tell the human resources specialists why you are calling and ask for their help in identifying job openings, both current and future.

Human resources personnel want to find the best applicants for open positions. Be prepared to state your qualifications, education, and experience. The more prepared you are when you call, the more interested they will be in helping you. Some agencies will take contact information and notify you, usually by e-mail, when vacancies occur.

Employment Service Centers

In some cities the OPM operates Employment Service Centers. You can call the centers directly to obtain information on job listings. The centers also feature kiosks with touch-screen monitors, which you can use in the same way as you would the Internet. Here is a list of federal employment Service Centers:

ATLANTA Service Center
75 Spring Street, SW, Suite 956
Atlanta, GA 30303
404-331-4588

CHICAGO Service Center
230 South Dearborn Street, DPN 30-3
Chicago, IL 60604
312-353-6234

DAYTON Service Center
200 West 2nd Street, Room 507
Dayton, OH 45402
937-225-2576

DENVER Service Center
12345 Alameda Parkway
P.O. Box 25167
Denver, CO 80225
303-236-8550

DETROIT Service Center
477 Michigan Avenue, Room 594
Detroit, MI 48226
313-226-2095

HONOLULU Service Center
300 Ala Moana Boulevard, Box 50028
Honolulu, HI 96850
808-541-2795

HUNTSVILLE Service Center
520 Wynn Drive, NW
Huntsville, AL 35816-3426
256-837-1271

KANSAS CITY Service Center
601 East 12th Street, Room 131
Kansas City, MO 64106
816-426-5705

NORFOLK Service Center
200 Granby Street, Room 500
Norfolk, VA 23510-1886
757-441-3373

PHILADELPHIA Service Center
600 Arch Street, Room 3400
Philadelphia, PA 19106
215-861-3031

RALEIGH Service Center
4407 Bland Road, Suite 200
Raleigh, NC 27609-6296
919-790-2817

SAN ANTONIO Service Center
8610 Broadway, Room 305
San Antonio, TX 78217
210-805-2423

SAN FRANCISCO Service Center
120 Howard Street, Room 735
San Francisco, CA 94105
415-281-7094

SAN JUAN Service Center
Torre de Plaza las Americas, Suite 1114
525 F.D. Roosevelt Avenue
San Juan, Puerto Rico 00918
787-766-5620

SEATTLE Service Center
700 5th Avenue, Suite 5950
Seattle, WA 98104-5012
206-553-0870

TWIN CITIES Service Center
One Federal Drive, Suite 596
Fort Snelling, MN 55111-4007
612-725-3437

WASHINGTON DC Service Center
1900 E Street, NW, Room 2458
Washington, DC 20415
202-606-2525

State Employment Services

Your state government also operates employment service centers and other employment services, including online listings. Look in the government pages of your telephone book for contact information, or go online and search under (your state's name).gov.

Job Fairs

If you would rather look for a job face-to-face rather than on the Internet, a federal job fair is the place for you. All the major agencies, as well as a large variety of positions, can be found at these recruitment fairs. These fairs travel the United States, so you should check online to find when the next fair will be in your area.

► OTHER AVENUES

Searching for a federal job, or any job, is a difficult and time-consuming task. It is important to investigate every possible avenue that might lead you to the job you want. If you have recently finished your education, your school might have a career center available for your job search. The quality and quantity of resources and information will vary from school to school, but they are there to make finding a job just a little easier. Be sure to ask for their help with your federal job search.

► NETWORKING WORKS

No matter how many sources you use to gather information in your federal job search, the agency with the most information about any particular job is the agency with that job opening. In some cases, an agency will never publicly list a vacancy at all. This is especially true for very desirable jobs, as the agency knows it will have no trouble filling those positions, often from within the agency.

Experienced and successful job applicants know that the single best way to get a job is to network. Networking involves identifying people who can help you and establishing and maintaining contacts with them.

Networking—Square One

A network is a group of people who can provide help, information, and support both during your job search and after you start your job. Networking for federal employment involves making contacts within the agency in which you wish to work and finding out from them about their work and the agency itself, as well as about positions available within the agency.

Think of a network as a web. You are at the center of the web. Everyone you know is on the next ring out from you, and everyone they know is on the ring out from that. If you are searching for a federal job, tell everyone from your family to your hairstylist about it; and ask if they know someone who can help you. Chances are, you know someone who knows someone who works in an agency you are interested in.

Don't be aggressive, but when you meet people or talk with people you already know, always mention your job search. The more people who know you are looking for a federal job, the better chance that someone will have a friend or relative in the government who could be a valuable contact for you. Most people enjoy helping others by making introductions; so don't be afraid to ask.

What Is a Contact?

A professional contact is someone who can help you pursue a career in your field of interest. Your best friend might offer moral support in your job search; but if your friend works in private healthcare and you want a federal job, he isn't going to be a great contact. Remember, a contact is not always someone you know directly.

There are rules of etiquette for establishing and maintaining professional contacts. Just as you treat your friends with consideration so they remain your friends, you must follow the rules of etiquette governing professional contacts.

Networking Etiquette

1. **Make an appointment.** Don't ambush your contact. If you want to discuss work, call or write to ask when it is most convenient for them to talk.
2. **Prepare questions.** Don't expect your contact to sit there and tell you everything you want to know. Use a list of meaningful questions that you would like the answers to.
3. **Don't get too personal.** Remember, depending on how well you know your contact, it is probably *not* appropriate to discuss, for example, his exact salary. You might ask him for a salary range for a certain position, but it is not polite to ask someone how much money they make. Also, unless you know your contact well, use Mr. or Ms. to address them.
4. **Steer clear of office gossip.** If your contact thinks it would be helpful for you to know about affairs and scandals at her office, politely tell her that this is not the kind of information that you are looking for. You might end up working there, and this sort of information might affect interactions with your coworkers.
5. **Keep it short.** Your contacts are helping you out, but that does not mean you should take advantage of their time. If you have prepared a targeted list of questions, you should be able to find out what you want and need to know in about 30 minutes.

6. **Take notes.** You are not going to be able to remember everything you discuss during an informational meeting. Bring a paper and pen with you to take *brief* notes as he or she talks, or wait until the meeting is over and spend a few minutes writing down what you learned and your thoughts about the meeting.

7. **Don't simply ask for a job.** The people in your network should not be expected to get you a job. They are to be utilized for information and possibly as references, but it is unreasonable to rely on him/her entirely to secure you a position.

8. **Say thank you.** If someone has taken the time to meet with you or to share his or her knowledge and experience with you, write a thank you note.

THREE STEPS TO NETWORKING SUCCESS

1. Prepare to network.
2. Make contacts.
3. Follow up with contacts.

▶ WHO DO YOU KNOW?

Now that you have prepared yourself and know some basic rules of networking, you can get started. First, regardless of what kind of job you are looking for, brainstorm a list of five to ten possible professional contacts. If you do not know someone's name, or don't know someone directly, write the name of the person who could introduce you.

HELPFUL HINT—TEN GOOD SOURCES FOR CONTACTS

1. Accountants (with clients in wide range of industries)
2. Bankers (with clients in wide range of industries)
3. Church/mosque/synagogue friends or clergy
4. School friends
5. Exercise club acquaintances
6. Family and friends
7. Hairdresser/barber/manicurist (with clients in wide range of industries)
8. Lawyers (with clients in wide range of industries)
9. Past teachers
10. High school or college friends

Contact all the people whose names you have written down. Tell them you are looking for a federal job and ask if they know a federal employee who might help you. If they will contact those people to let them know you are going to call, that makes your job easier.

Prepare Your Questions

Before you meet with a contact, take a few minutes and brainstorm ten to twenty questions you think would be helpful to ask. Here are some questions to get you started, but try to think of others that are specific to the work you are interested in:

Where did you find this (or any other) job?

How did you first get started at this agency?

How long have you worked at this field?

How long have you had this specific job?

Have you had other jobs at other agencies?

What are your typical daily duties?

Do your duties change often or do you do the same thing every day?

What skills are most important in this job?

How many hours per week do you work?

What was the hiring process like at this agency?

Have you had to update your training or skills since you started?

How has this agency changed in the last 2–3 years?

How has your specific job changed in the last 2–3 years?

What is the career path for this job (for example: promotions)?

What do you like most about your job/agency?

What do you like least about your job/agency?

Follow Up

After you have met with or talked to your contacts, you will need to follow up. Following up is one of the most important things you can do to show people that you are serious about finding a job and that you are responsible. Understand that if someone asks you to call them next week, or if you set up an appointment for later that week with someone, that these are *commitments*. Your reputation for reliability and responsibility is on the line every time you are asked, or offer, to do something. You won't remember everything, so write things in your planner or calendar so that you don't forget to do them.

Thank You Notes

One thing you are never asked to do, but always *should* do after any informational meeting, is to write a thank you note. If someone has taken the time to provide you with information, you should take the time to say thank you. Of course when you are leaving a meeting you should *say* thank you, but *writing* a note shows an extra bit of effort and certainly can make you stand out in his or her mind.

A thank you note can be typed on your personal letterhead or neatly handwritten in blue or black ink on clean unlined paper or on a neutral blank card. Write a rough draft of your thank you note so that the final draft will be free of any writing or spelling errors.

Grow Your Network

As you get better at networking, you will be meeting more and more people in your field. The more people you meet and establish as contacts, the more your contact list can grow. After you have established one contact, you can ask if that person might be able to put you in touch with other people in their agency. This will expand your contact list and the range of your job search, maximizing your chances for finding the job you want.

▶ SUMMARY

Yes, looking for federal employment is hard work. But it's hard work that you want to be doing. You know the harder you work at finding employment, the sooner that dream job becomes yours.

The most important thing you need to learn from this chapter is that there are many avenues to finding a federal job, and you must take all of them in order to succeed. Now you have all the information you need in order to locate the job openings you would like to fill. In the next chapter you will learn how to understand federal job announcements, to determine if you meet the qualification requirements, and to begin the application process.

CHAPTER

3

How to Apply for a Federal Job

The process of applying for a federal job is unlike any other job application experience. Federal agencies are very particular about what information they want from you, and sometimes it seems as though no two agencies are alike in their requirements. They want a lot of information, and they want it presented in a certain way, which will vary according to the agency and the type of job you are applying for.

The first hurdle you have to clear is the job announcement itself. Federal job listings are long, detailed, and often confusing at first glance. You may find yourself tempted to give up before you even begin the application process. Do not worry, though. This chapter will introduce you to the intricacies of the federal job announcement.

After you have learned how to decipher what the job announcement says, you still may be confused about whether or not you are qualified for the position. In this chapter you will learn how to determine which jobs you can expect to successfully apply for.

As you zero in on the job or jobs that are right for you, this chapter will provide you with invaluable information about the application process. You will learn how to complete the various forms that may be required, the exams you may have to take, as well as how to compose and post your resume online at the federal job site, www.usajobs.opm.gov. You will see that the federal application process is not as hard as it looks.

▶ WHAT IS IN A LISTING?

If you are used to looking at a newspaper or magazine, or any non-governmental source of job listings, you could be shocked to discover the amount of information a federal job listing contains. It may seem overwhelming at first glance, but the great thing about federal job announcements is that they really take the guesswork out of your job application process.

Anyone who has done much job hunting has had the experience of finding a listing for what seemed like the perfect job, sending in a resume, and never hearing anything from the hiring company, much less getting an interview. The frustrating thing about that is you never know why you were not selected. Chances are, the three-line advertisement for the job omitted crucial information that would have helped you tailor your resume to fit the posted opening.

A federal job announcement contains much detailed information about the duties of a listed position; and it tells you what qualifications are required and how your application will be evaluated. Then, it tells you how to apply. Even though it may take you quite awhile to wade through all that information and complete your detailed application, you will be well informed about the job and unlikely to waste your time applying for a job for which you will not be considered.

▶ HOW DO I START?

As you learned in Chapter 2, the best place to find federal job listings is the Office of Personnel Management (OPM). OPM operates a voice-response job hotline system at 478-757-3000 (TDD 478-744-2299). The easiest, cheapest way to access OPM's extensive job listings, though, is by going online to www.usajobs.opm.gov. Remember that if you do not have a computer, you can use one at the public library for free.

You probably have a pretty good idea of the type(s) of job(s) you are interested in and qualified for. If you are thinking about a career change, you may want to utilize OPM's Career Interests Center, which can be accessed by clicking on the link found on the site's Home Page.

OPM'S CAREER INTERESTS CENTER

You can explore how to translate your private sector experience into a federal job by going to http://career.usajobs.opm.gov/cw/list.asp and clicking on "Match Federal Jobs to Private Sector Jobs." You can select a federal job that interests you and see a list of private sector jobs that may qualify you for that job.

▶ UNDERSTANDING THE LISTING

Once you have located a listing that interests you, it is time to look at the job in depth. When you search for jobs on the OPM website, the first information you will see about a job is a summary of important information. It will look something like this:

Opening Date	Job Summary	Agency	Locations
Oct. 1, 2004	<u>SUPERVISORY POLICE OFFICER</u> **Who May Apply:** Status / Federal Civil Service Employees, Public **Pay Plan:** ZP-0083-08 **Appointment Term:** Permanent **Job Status:** Full Time **Closing Date:** 10/17/2004 **Salary:** From 36,255 to 47,132 USD per year	Smithsonian	US-DC-WASHINGTON

Posting Date

The date in the upper left corner is the date the listing was posted. When you run a job search, the most recently posted jobs will be at the top of the search results. That means the jobs at the bottom of the search results will have been posted longer. They may be closing soon.

HELPFUL HINT—IT'S A MATTER OF TIME

When you have more than one job returned in a search, scroll down to the end of the search results first. You may discover a job that closes in a few days. If you apply to the newer listings first, you may miss out on the perfect position!

Position Title

The job title is found just to the right of the posting date. It is in all capital letters and is underlined. In this case, it is <u>SUPERVISORY POLICE OFFICER</u>. Clicking on the job title will take you to the full-length job listing. Before you do that, though, look at the other information in the job summary to make sure this is a job you are interested in learning more about.

Agency and Location

To the right of the job title you will find the employing agency, in this case the Smithsonian Institution, and the actual location of the job. This job is in Washington, DC.

Who May Apply

If you are not already a federal employee, the word you are looking for next to the *Who May Apply* heading is *public*. In this sample listing, you can see that federal civil service employees as well as the general public may apply.

Pay Plan

As you may recall from Chapter 1, there are several types of pay plans in the federal government. The GS and WS plans are the most common. The ZP plan referred to in this listing is a pay plan for those in the Scientific and Engineering career path. The last two numbers denote the grade (08) of the position within the ZP plan. As you will see, it is not necessary to know the details of a particular pay plan to get a sense of the salary range.

Federal job listings often state which pay plan levels may apply to a particular job. For example, a particular job may list pay plan levels from GS5–GS7. That would mean that the job would probably start as a GS5, and that an employee could achieve GS7 status, with its commensurate boost in pay range, while remaining in the same position.

Appointment Term and Job Status

Many jobs are temporary appointments, and that will be noted after the Appointment Term heading. In this case, the job is a permanent appointment. It is also full-time, not part-time.

Closing Date

This is the heading to check to see when you must have completed your application. It is a good idea to allow several days for the system to process your application, so be sure to apply at least a week or so before the closing date.

Salary

The salary for this position will be somewhere between $36,255 per year and $47,132 per year. Normally, your starting salary will be toward the lower end of the salary range; and you will receive raises until you reach the top of the range or earn a promotion.

Should I Learn More?

If you have determined from the brief announcement that you are 1) eligible to apply for the job, and 2) interested in the job, after learning of its location, appointment term/status, and salary, then you are ready to learn more about the position. To see a much more detailed description, including information that will guide you in your application, click on the job title, in this case SUPERVISORY POLICE OFFICER.

VACANCY ANNOUNCEMENT
SMITHSONIAN INSTITUTION

Vacancy Announcement Number:	03SP-1359
Opening Date:	Wednesday, October 01, 2004
Closing Date:	Friday, October 17, 2004
Position:	**SUPERVISORY POLICE OFFICER**
Series & Grade:	ZP-0083-08
Salary:	36,255.00–47,132.00 USD Annually
Duty Locations:	1 vacancy - WASHINGTON, DC
Remarks:	REISSUED TO CHANGE SELECTIVE FACTORS AND TO EXTEND CLOSING DATE. THE PERSON SELECTED FOR THIS POSITION MAY BE SUBJECT TO AN 18-MONTH PROBATIONARY PERIOD FOR SUPERVISORS. RELOCATION EXPENSES WILL NOT BE PAID.

Who May Apply

All candidates may apply including individuals with a disability with eligibility under a special appointing authority and veterans who are preference eligibles or who have been separated from the armed forces under honorable conditions after three years or more of continuous active service. (If a competitive list of eligibles is requested, the applications of non-status candidates who meet the minimum qualification for the position will be referred to the Delegated Examining Unit (DEU) for consideration. Status candidates and candidates eligible under a special appointing authority, who wish to be rated under both merit placement and DEU's competitive procedures, must submit two complete applications. If only one application is received, it will be considered under the merit placement program.) The Smithsonian provides reasonable accommodations to applicants with disabilities. If you need a reasonable accommodation for the application/hiring process, please call 202-275-1102 (voice) or 202-275-1110 (TTY).

Under Executive Order 11935, only United States citizens and nationals (residents of American Samoa and Swains Island) may compete for civil service jobs.

Additional Duty Location Info
NATIONAL ZOOLOGICAL PARK FACILITIES

Major Duties
The incumbent is responsible for the maintenance of law and order, prevention of crime, safe guarding of government property, detection and investigation of violations of Federal and District of Columbia law, preservation of peace, arrest of violators, enforcement of rules and regulations within the Park. Supervises all Police Officers assigned to his or her area. Assigns personnel to "beats." Supervises or leads the activities of the police force. Responsible for the proper conduct, appearance, and discipline of the force. Investigates complaints of crimes and accidents within the Park. Trains personnel in accepted police techniques in the enforcement of regulations, laws and ordinances, and range firing. The incum-

bent is responsible for patrol and enforcement of District of Columbia laws and regulations in the area immediately surrounding the park. To perform this function incumbent may be required to successfully complete courses with the Metropolitan Police Department and become certified to patrol in accordance with the agreement.

Qualifications Required

One year of specialized experience at least equivalent to the Grade 7 level. Acceptable specialized experience includes experience that provided knowledge of a body of basic law and regulations, law enforcement operations, practices, and techniques and involved responsibility for maintaining order and protecting life and property. Creditable experience may have been gained through work on a police force, through service as a military police officer, or comparable experience involving responsibility for maintaining order and protecting life.

How You Will Be Evaluated

Selective Factors: (Applicants must meet all of these mandatory requirements in order to be considered qualified to compete for a position.)

1. Knowledge of District of Columbia and Federal criminal and civil laws and regulations and practices as they pertain to enforcement of criminal codes, statues, traffic laws, and regulations relating to public safety and/or park security measures.
2. Skill in enforcement of Federal, state, or municipal criminal laws as demonstrated by experience as a police officer with a Federal, state, or municipal police force.
3. Ability to supervise including support of EEO goals.

Quality Ranking Factors: (These factors are not mandatory to be considered for a position, but will be used to determine who are the highest qualified candidates among those who meet the selective factors.)

1. Knowledge of Federal and District of Columbia laws, rules and regulations in order to enforce law enforcement practices as they pertain to public safety and park security measures.
2. Knowledge of police methods, procedures, and techniques as they pertain to arrests, search and seizure, use of force, and crowd control.
3. Knowledge of District of Columbia criminal codes, statues, ordinances and traffic laws and regulations.
4. Skill in preparing and conducting in-service training programs.
5. Skill in oral communications (e.g. demonstrating tact and diplomacy in dealing with others).
6. Ability to supervise including support of EEO goals.

Applicants meeting basic eligibility requirements will be rated and ranked on the knowledges, skills, and abilities, and other characteristics (KSAs) required to perform the duties of the position. Please review KSAs carefully. Include in the write-ups such things as experience in and out of Federal service that gave you the specific knowledge, skill or ability; objectives of your work; and evidence of your success (such as accomplishments, awards received, etc.)

How to Apply

1. The Smithsonian Institution does not require a standard application form, but we need certain information to evaluate your qualifications. You may apply using a resume, the Optional Application for Federal Employment, or any other written application form you choose, including an SF-171, Application for Federal Employment. Note: If you use an SF-171, do not answer questions 38-47. Job finalists will be asked to complete a Declaration for Federal Employment. The information on this form will be used to determine suitability for Federal employment and to authorize a background investigation, if required.)

2. Clearly describe in your resume or application your work experience, education and/or training as it relates to this vacancy. It is very important that you fully address how your work experience and education/training meet both the specialized experience requirement and the selective factors. This information will be used to determine whether or not you are qualified for this vacancy. Selective factors establish qualifications to be eligible to compete for the position. Quality Ranking Factors are not mandatory but are used to determine who are the highest qualified candidates among those eligible to compete for the position. Therefore, it is to your benefit to provide a full description of your experience and education/training relative to the job requirements of this vacancy.

3. Current federal employees should submit a copy of their most recent annual performance appraisal and a copy of their most recent complete SF-50.

Applications must be received by the closing date and may be submitted in the following ways:

Mail: Smithsonian Institution, Office of Human Resources, P. O. Box 50638, Washington, DC 20091.
Fax: 202-275-1114
Hand Deliver or FEDEX: 750 Ninth Street, N. W. Suite 6100, Washington, DC 20560.

To obtain information on the Federal Hiring Process, hear about other Smithsonian vacancies, or request vacancy announcements, an Optional Application for Federal Employment (OF-612), or an SF-171, call our automated Jobline at 202-287-3102 (accessible 24 hours, 7 days a week).

For further information please call 202-275-1117 (voice) or 202-275-1110 (TTY).

SMITHSONIAN INSTITUTION FEDERAL POSITIONS
YOUR RESUME OR APPLICATION MUST INCLUDE THE FOLLOWING INFORMATION RELEVANT TO THIS VACANCY.

Job Information
Announcement number, job title, and grade level(s) of the job for which you are applying.

Personal Information
Full name, mailing address, and zip code, home and work telephone numbers (With area code), and Social Security Number.
Citizenship (Provide country or countries of citizenship).
Veterans' preference, if any. (Attach DD-214 Submit SF-15 if claiming 10-point preference.)
Competitive status, if any. (If you are a current or former federal employee, attach a copy of your most recent SF-50, Notification of Personnel Action).

Eligibility under special authority, i.e., applicants with a disability, including veterans, or any other applicants eligible for non-competitive appointment. (Indicate the basis for your eligibility and attach supporting documentation.)

Education

High school—name, city, state, zip code, and date of diploma or GED.

College(s)—for each college you attended, give: name of school, location (city, state, and zip code), credit hours earned (semester or quarter), and type and year of degree(s), if any. To qualify based on education, submit a copy of your transcript or list of courses (with credit hours), major(s), and grade-point average or class rank.

Work Experience

Describe your paid and non-paid work experience that is related to the job for which you are applying. Provide the following for each job listed:

Job title (Give series and grade if a federal job.)

Name of organization, supervisor's name, and telephone number

Starting and ending dates of job (month and year)

Average number of hours worked per week

Salary

A description of your duties, responsibilities, and accomplishments

Indicate if we may not contact your current supervisor

Other Qualifications

Job-related training courses (title and year)

Job-related skills (for example, languages and skill level, computer software/hardware, tools, machinery, typing and/or steno speeds)

Job-related certificates and licenses (current only)

Job-related honors, awards, and special accomplishments. (for example, publications, memberships in professional or honor societies, leadership and public speaking activities, and performance awards—give dates but do not send documents unless requested)

Additional Information

U.S. citizenship is required for most federal positions. The Immigration Reform and Control Act of 1986 requires employers to hire only individuals who are eligible to work in the United States. Upon reporting for work, an individual will be expected to present proper evidence establishing employability.

Where applicable, time-in-grade, time after competitive appointment, and qualification requirements must be met within thirty (30) days of the closing date.

Before hiring, candidates will be requested to complete a Declaration for Federal Employment to determine suitability for Federal employment, to authorize a background investigation, and to certify the accuracy of their application. Most Smithsonian positions require fingerprinting of employees hired.

Applications submitted in postage-paid government envelopes will not be accepted. If you omit information requested on this announcement, your application may be rated ineligible.

Other Information

WORKING CONDITION AND PHYSICAL REQUIREMENTS: Majority of work is performed outside in a variety of weather conditions. Requires moderate to arduous physical exertion including prolonged walking and standing. The following medical requirements apply to all applicants: good near and distant vision, ability to distinguish basic colors, and ability to hear the conversational voice. Work will also be in proximity with wild animals. Must qualify annually with departmental firearm. Must possess a valid motor vehicle operator's permit from the District of Columbia or its immediate adjacent states.

SPECIAL CONDITIONS OF EMPLOYMENT: The incumbent is required to carry a firearm and qualify annually in accordance with Smithsonian Institution polices. Subject to work any three shifts, including Saturday, Sunday, or Holidays on a regular and recurring basis. The position which may be filled from this vacancy announcement has been identified as a Testing Designated under the Drug-Free Workplace Program. All applicants tentatively selected for this position shall be required to submit to urinalysis to screen for illegal drug use prior to appointment. Satisfactory completion of the drug test is a condition of placement and/or employment in the position and the incumbent of this position is, thereafter, subject to Random Drug Testing. This is an emergency position.

All Federal employees are required by PL 104-134 to have federal payments made by Direct Deposit.

Your Social Security Number (SSN) is requested under the authority of Executive Order 9397 to uniquely identify your records from those of other applicants who may have the same name. As allowed by law or Presidential directive, your SSN is used to seek information about you from employers, schools, banks, and others who may know you. Failure to provide your SSN on your application materials will result in your application not being processed.

You must clearly identify your claim for veteran's preference on your application.

5-POINT PREFERENCE. A 5-point preference is granted to veterans who served prior to 1976 and served at least six months on active duty. Those who served after 1980 and 1982 must have served at least two years on active duty.

A 5-point preference is also granted to veterans who served on active duty during the Gulf War from August 2, 1990 through January 2, 1992. The law grants preference to anyone who is otherwise eligible and who served on active duty during this period regardless of where the person served or for how long. Otherwise eligible means that the person must have been released from the service under honorable conditions and must have served a minimum of two years on active duty, or if a reservist, must have served the full period for which called to active duty.

If you are claiming a 5-point veteran preference please provide a DD-214, Certificate of Release or Discharge from Active Duty, or other proof of entitlement. Tentative preference will be granted in the absence of the paperwork.

10-POINT PREFERENCE. You may be entitled to a 10-point veteran preference if you are a disabled veteran; you have received the Purple Heart; you are the spouse or mother of a 100% disabled veteran; or, you are the widow, widower, or mother of a deceased veteran. If you are claiming 10-point veteran preference, you will need to submit an SF-15, Application for 10-point Veteran Preference, plus the proof required by that form.

This is a permanent, career-conditional appointment. Selectee will be eligible for health and life insurance, annual (vacation) and sick leave, and will be covered under the Federal Employees Retirement System.

EEO Statements

Background Survey Questionnaire

PLEASE FORWARD THIS FORM TO: Smithsonian Institution, Office of Equal Employment and Minority Affairs, 750 Ninth Street, N.W., Suite 8100 Washington, DC 20560-0921

For additional information on this vacancy, contact:

Smithsonian Jobline

Phone: 202-287-3102

Fax: 202-275-1114

▶ THE VACANCY ANNOUNCEMENT

As you can see from reading this vacancy announcement, no detail is spared. The first few headings of the vacancy announcement add only a little new information to the brief description you have already seen. Here is an examination of the introductory sections of the full announcement.

Vacancy Announcement Number

The vacancy announcement number is an important piece of new information. You must include this number on any application form you submit, including your resume. In fact, if you are not submitting an electronic resume or form, it is a good idea to make sure this number is on *each page* of your application documents.

Repetition of the Essentials

The opening and closing dates, the position title, the series and grade of the job, and the duty location repeat, for the most part, the information in the brief description. One additional bit of information is that there is only one vacancy with this particular title.

Remarks

In the remarks section you learn that this job has been previously posted. It was posted again (*reissued*) in order to change *selective factors* and extend the closing date. Selective factors are the qualifications by which applicants will be evaluated. For some reason, about which you can only speculate, the previously posted selective factors were deemed inadequate or superfluous and so new ones have been added and/or old ones deleted.

You also learn that there *may* be an 18-month probationary period for the successful applicant. That means there also may not be a probationary period. Additionally, if you must relocate to take the job, your moving expenses will not be paid.

Who May Apply

This section is an expansion of the brief announcement. Any U.S. citizen or national is eligible to apply, including those with disabilities (more about this in a subsequent section) and veterans. The Delegated Examining Unit (DEU) mentioned in this section is a unit within the hiring agency, which has an agreement with OPM that it will do its own competitive hiring. The DEU, then, is the group that will be ranking candidates for the job.

In the context of this paragraph, a special appointing authority is one that assists individuals with disabilities in obtaining federal employment. A status candidate is one who either is currently serving under a career-type civil-service appointment or who formerly served under such an appointment. Neither of these candidate categories is required to go through the competitive procedures, although such candidates may opt to do so.

Additional Duty Location Info

In this section, you discover that the job site is the National Zoological Park. The successful applicant will be working at the National Zoo.

Major Duties

For the first time, you get a look at the actual responsibilities of the successful candidate for this job. When you read the *Major Duties* section, pay close attention to the words used to describe the duties, especially the verbs, the action words.

In this description, you learn that the successful candidate will *assign* personnel, *supervise or lead* activities, *investigate* complaints, and so on. It is essential that your application use exactly the same words as the ones in the announcement. What other action words can you find in this description of major duties? In Chapter 6, you will learn how to quickly and accurately match the verbs in your application to the verbs used in federal job announcements.

Qualifications Required

Notice that, even though this is a grade level 8 position, you are not required to have experience at this level. The announcement notes that you must have specialized experience (experience appropriate to this job) at grade level 7. The announcement tells you what kinds of experience will be considered appropriate.

How You Will Be Evaluated

This is perhaps the most crucial area of the vacancy announcement. It is divided into two sections. The first section tells you the mandatory requirements (*selective factors*) that the successful candidate must meet. There are three of them.

Note that the first mandatory requirement is knowledge of District of Columbia and Federal laws, codes, statutes, etc. as they apply to public safety or park security. This means that if you cannot demonstrate this knowledge, you need not apply, as it is a mandatory requirement for the job. Now you see that the pool of potentially successful applicants is smaller than you might have imagined. If you are a police officer in Iowa without any knowledge of District of Columbia and Federal laws, it will be pointless for you to apply for this position. On the other hand, if you are a District of Columbia police officer, you will want to keep reading the announcement.

This section is also your introduction to the concept of Knowledge, Skills, and Abilities (KSAs). As the next chapter and subsequent chapters will elaborate on, this concept must be mastered if you wish to be hired for a federal job. Notice that the three mandatory requirements are presented as one area of *knowledge*, one *skill*, and one *ability*.

If you meet the mandatory requirements and keep reading, you will see that the next section of the announcement sets forth the *Quality Ranking Factors*. These qualifications are not mandatory. They will be used to decide which of the qualifying candidates will rank most highly in the competitive process.

Notice that, again, these factors are presented in terms of Knowledge, Skills, and Abilities. Again, the first factor is specific knowledge of District of Columbia laws. When the concluding paragraph of this section says that you must read these KSAs carefully, it is giving you valuable advice. Approach this section of any vacancy announcement carefully; comb it for useful information. Make notes of the specific language used in the announcement so that you can mirror it back in your application.

How to Apply

This section mentions several federal forms that may be used to apply for this and other positions. Do not be distracted by the variety of forms mentioned. The essence of this section is that you can use any type of written application form you want to use.

The SF-171 is a form for those who are already federal employees and who have this standard form (SF) already prepared. The Declaration for Federal Employment is a box and bubble type of form that is completed when an offer of employment is made.

The Optional Application for Federal Employment may also be referred to as OF-612. It looks much like other application forms you have seen, with little boxes for your responses to standard prompts relating to work experience, education, and so forth. A resume, in which you expound on how you possess the KSAs required for the position, is a much better format for your application.

The second paragraph in this section reminds you how important it is to *fully address* the selective factors and the specialized experience requirement for this position. You must understand the requirements of the position and you must fully address how your work experience and education meet those requirements. This match between the job's requirements and your KSAs is the essence of your rating in comparison to other applicants.

The form mentioned in the third paragraph, the SF-50, is also known as a Notification of Personnel Action. It applies only to current federal employees.

The remainder of this section tells you what additional information must be included in your application. Again, be certain that you include all the requested information about yourself, your education, your work experience, and other qualifications.

Other Information

In the paragraph titled *Working Condition and Physical Requirements*, you find another series of potentially exclusionary qualifications. No discrimination against individuals with disabilities is allowed in the federal government; however, if an individual cannot perform the essential duties of the job, that individual cannot qualify for the position. Here you see that *moderate to arduous physical exertion including prolonged walking and standing* is required. Additionally, successful applicants must be able to hear conversations and have the ability to see well and distinguish basic colors. If you cannot meet these conditions, you are unlikely to be a successful candidate.

Under *Special Conditions of Employment*, you learn that you must carry a firearm and qualify to use it. You will also be tested for illegal drug use before you are employed and at random intervals thereafter. In subsequent paragraphs you learn that certain veterans of the armed forces are entitled to a five-point preference in the competitive ratings. Disabled veterans and certain survivors of deceased veterans are eligible for a ten-point preference.

EEO Statements

Finally, you are asked to complete a form that asks about your racial and ethnic identity. The form, which also asks how you learned about the vacancy, is used only for statistical purposes and does not affect your application in any way. All government agencies have Equal Employment Opportunities (EEO).

▶ BUT I'M NOT A POLICE OFFICER

Of course, every federal vacancy announcement is different. As you learned in Chapter 2, not every job opening is listed on OPM's website; and a vacancy announcement on another agency's website will be laid out differently. The format may vary, but each federal job listing will contain much of the same detailed-type information you saw in the police officer listing.

There are also crucial ways in which most federal vacancy announcements are alike. Even if you see a short listing in a newspaper or magazine, there still exists a longer and more detailed announcement that will let you know very specifically whether or not you are qualified for that position.

▶ HOW CAN I BE SURE I'M QUALIFIED?

As you saw in the vacancy announcement for a Supervisory Police Officer, there is a section titled *Qualifications Required.* This section is present in every federal announcement. Sometimes it is straightforward and clear. Sometimes it can be a little less so.

There are two main areas of qualification that may be required for any given job. They are **education** and **experience**. Where the qualification requirements can get a bit tricky is in the many situations that allow various combinations of education and experience. With a bit of patience, though, you can determine exactly what the requirements are for any given job.

Education

Many government jobs have some kind of educational requirement. It may be a high school diploma or GED. It may some college courses or a college degree. It could be graduate work in a specific field, or it may be specialized training such as business school or technical training. One good point is that the federal government is generous in giving credit for post-high school education that did not lead to a degree.

In general, you can estimate how much or how little education is required by looking at the pay plan level. For a GS-2 level job or its equivalent, for example, you can qualify as a high school graduate with no work experience. If you are a college graduate without work experience, you will generally be eligible for a GS-5 level job. If you maintained a B average, you can usually start at the GS-7 pay scale. Higher pay plan levels may require graduate level education.

Professional jobs, such as accountant or engineer, require specific courses of study related to the positions. If this is the case, it will be noted in the vacancy announcement. Many other jobs, however, at the GS-5 level and above, do not require a specific field of study.

Experience

General Experience

For most jobs, other than some professional jobs, you do not have to have college credentials. You need only have appropriate work experience. At the lowest pay scale, the GS-2 level, you can qualify without a high school diploma and with as little as three months of general work experience. General experience is work that is not necessarily related to the position for which you are applying. Below the GS-7 pay scale, positions are considered to be entry level and may require no experience, or a limited amount of general work experience.

Specialized Experience

If you do not have a high school diploma, you generally must have at least a year of specialized experience to qualify for a GS-5 level position. Even with a diploma, most GS-7 level jobs and above require at least some specialized experience. Specialized experience must be closely related to the work you will perform in the job for which you are applying. Such experience will equip you with the knowledge, skills, and abilities you need to successfully perform the duties of the position. It should be noted at this point that sometimes qualifying experience is not paid work experience at all, but volunteer work or even life experience.

However, appropriate specialized experience must be at a level of responsibility that corresponds to the level below the one for which you wish to be considered. You saw the Police Officer announcement, which was a grade level 8. For that job you needed at least a year of specialized experience equivalent to a grade level 7.

Education and Experience Combinations

For most federal jobs, various combinations of post-high school education and experience will qualify you for a particular grade level. There is no one formula that covers all government positions. The important thing to remember is that you must demonstrate the required qualifications very specifically in your application documents.

Look It Up Online

The best way to determine whether or not your particular combination of experience and education qualifies you for a specific job is to go online to www.opm.gov/qualifications/SEC-III/A/num-NDX.HTM. This is a page on the OPM website titled *Group Qualification Standards for GS Positions* and subtitled *Numerical Index by Series.* Find the series that covers the position(s) you are interested in and click on it. You may remember that the series are identified by a three or four digit number as well as by title. The series cover such areas as General Administrative; Clerical and Office Services; Education; Supply; and Transportation. When you click on one of the series titles, it takes you to a page that will tell you the qualification standards for individual positions within that series.

Get It On Paper

Your application will be rated, based on your demonstrated qualifications, and you will receive a numerical score, just as you would with a written exam. The person looking at your application will usually score it based solely on how well it meets the stated qualification requirements. If you score a 94 and someone else gets a 95, you probably won't get the job, even though you may actually be the better candidate. Chapter 4 and the remainder of this book will teach you how to maximize your education and experience throughout the application process.

▶ WHAT ABOUT EXAMINATIONS?

You may have heard that you have to take an exam to qualify for civil service. There was a time when that was almost universally true, but not anymore. The majority of government jobs no longer require a written examination. As you learned in the previous section, your application is scored as though it were an exam, with 100 being a perfect score. There are, however, still jobs that do require you to take some sort of exam.

Entry Level Positions

Many jobs at the GS-2, GS-3, and GS-4 level still require tests. These may be written exams, performance exams, or both. To qualify as a clerk-typist, for example, you may need to take a written exam designed to insure you have the literacy level necessary to perform clerical work. This may be the Clerical and Administrative Support Exam or another exam selected by the hiring agency. In some cases, you will be allowed to substitute a work sample for a written exam. You may also have to pass a typing exam, which is a kind of performance exam. In certain cases, you will be able to substitute a certificate of proficiency from an accredited institution for the performance exam. Technical aid jobs at the GS-2 and GS-3 level often require written tests as well.

Other Jobs Requiring Exams

Some jobs require aptitude exams. The Postal Service, for example, administers aptitude exams to most prospective employees. Some jobs require physical exams prior to taking the position. If a job requires that you demonstrate certain kinds of knowledge, you may be tested to determine the level of your knowledge. A prospective Border Patrol Agent, for example, will be tested for language proficiency, as well as being required to take a written exam. Many administrative positions require an exam known as Administrative Careers with America (ACWA). Most Investigation positions (series 1800–1899) require some sort of written exam. The best way to know if you will be required to take an examination is to go to the previously mentioned website (www.opm.gov/qualifications/SEC-III/A/num-NDX.HTM) and look up the specific job you are interested in.

You should be aware that there are also exceptions to examination requirements. Direct-hire appointments are available through the Outstanding Scholar program, for students with high grade point averages. Examination waivers may also be obtained by an agency if labor market shortages exist for a particular job or in the event of other special circumstances. This information will almost always be contained in the detailed vacancy announcement; so never assume anything, but always read to find out.

▶ SUMMARY

In this chapter you have learned how to read a federal vacancy announcement. You know what information is in each section, and you know how to find the language that tells you what qualifications you need. That means you are halfway to your goal of landing the perfect government job.

Your next step is completing the perfect application, and that is not as hard as it sounds. Once you can read and understand the vacancy announcement, you can use what you read to write the resume or application that will get you the job. The remainder of this book is devoted to helping you do just that.

KSAs and the CCAR Model

In this chapter you will start to learn about the process that can most enhance your chances for success in securing a federal job. The process is the writing of KSAs, and KSAs are the most vital component of your federal job application. Essentially, your KSAs (Knowledge, Skills, and Abilities) determine whether or not you will be identified as a better candidate than the other applicants.

The vast majority of federal jobs now require you to write KSAs when you apply. If you do not know the best way to write these accounts of your qualifications, you may not be maximizing your qualifications properly. KSAs are like so many other things: hard to do when you don't know how; easy once you learn.

Some people get confused about the KSAs. If they are submitting a resume, isn't that the same thing, they wonder? In short, the answer is no. Think of your resume as a summary of your experience, education, and training. Even though you may list your job title and main duties, your resume cannot reveal much about you and your abilities. That's the job of your KSAs, to demonstrate by the use of examples, that you possess the qualifications for the job. These examples must be concisely written and informative, and each one must be submitted on a separate sheet of paper.

HELPFUL HINT—THINK IT THROUGH

Think of KSAs as written interview questions. If you were asked a KSA question in a job interview, how would you respond? The advantage to writing your KSA responses is that you have lots of time to think about your answers!

▶ KNOWLEDGE, SKILLS, AND ABILITIES—KSAs

The Job Analysis

When a federal job vacancy occurs, the agency that needs to hire a new worker performs or updates a job analysis for the vacant position. A job analysis is the systematic study of a job, the identification of the tasks performed in the job, and the linkage of the tasks performed to the competencies required for performance of these tasks.

The Vacancy Announcement

When the agency has determined both what tasks are performed in the job and the competencies required to perform the tasks, it can confidently write the vacancy announcement, setting forth the minimum requirements for the job (Selective Factors) and the desired but optional requirements (Quality Ranking Factors).

How to Respond

When you respond to the vacancy announcement, your responses to the Selective and Quality Ranking Factors take the form of KSAs. KSA stands for Knowledge, Skills, and Abilities. Your KSA responses must demonstrate your ability to successfully perform the tasks required in the position.

In order to successfully perform the required tasks, you will need **knowledge**, defined as the body of information, usually factual or procedural in nature you need to perform a job function. You may also need **skills**, defined as measurable competencies to perform specific mental, manual, or verbal manipulations. And you will need **abilities**, the competencies to perform observable activities or behaviors that result in observable products, similar to those required in the job.

The set of Knowledge, Skills, and Abilities required in order to perform a particular job is the set of KSAs you must demonstrate in your application. Typically there will be between three and eight KSAs you must address in an application. You will want to write between one and one and a half pages about each of the required KSAs. Don't be wordy, though; keep it brief and to the point. Be sure to put each KSA on a separate sheet of paper.

THREE WORDS OF CLARIFICATION

Knowledge, Skills, Abilities (KSAs) can be used to refer either to the qualifications required for a particular job or to the responses written to address those qualifications. KSA may be used interchangeably in either sense.

Selective Factors

When you write a KSA for a selective factor, keep in mind that the selective factors are used to screen out unqualified applicants. You will be deemed qualified or unqualified for the job based on your KSAs for these position requirements. Selective factors are essential for success in the position. If an applicant does not possess competence in each selective factor, he or she is considered unable to perform the job.

Selective factors are almost always specific technical competencies, such as knowledge of a particular set of practices and techniques (see the Police Officer announcement in Chapter 3), experience with particular computer programs, or facility with a certain language. They are not the things that can reasonably be learned on the job in a short time, usually requiring extensive experience or education to be successfully performed.

As you can see, the Selective Factor KSAs are extremely important. If your KSAs are not evaluated as satisfying the requirements, you will not receive any further consideration for the job. Examine the Selective Factors closely to determine the exact proficiency levels required, and carefully document those proficiencies in your KSAs.

Quality Ranking Factors

Once you are determined to meet the basic requirements for the job, the KSA examiners turn to your KSAs for the Quality Ranking Factors. These factors are designed to fine-tune the level of proficiency each individual applicant can bring to the job.

What this means is that your KSA responses will be examined with an eye toward determining exactly how effective you can be in the job you are applying for. Your responses will be rated against the other candidates' responses, and you will be placed on a rank ordered list of eligible candidates.

Your Quality Ranking Factor KSAs will be searched for such details as the hierarchical level of your current or previous job, your successful performance on that job, your increasing levels of responsibility, and the scope and breadth of your competencies. These are not the type of details you may be used to revealing on a two-page resume, so it may take some getting used to. Once you have done the necessary work to uncover these things about your employment history and education, however, you will be glad to have done it.

HELPFUL HINT—ARE YOU QUALIFIED?

The Selective Factors and the Quality Ranking Factors are the standards against which all applicants are measured. The more closely you can match your responses to the qualifications set forth in the vacancy announcement, the more likely you are to be considered a highly qualified applicant.

Show Me the Evidence

The reason KSAs have become so common in government applications is that they are considered to be good predictors of successful performance in government jobs. The collective evidence of your experience, education, and training must show that you meet the requirements of the position, which have been determined by the job analysis.

In writing each KSA, first decide whether you have a single strong illustration of the competency, or set of competencies, required. If you do have one good example, devote your entire page to page and a half to that example. If not, you may choose to write about two or three accomplishments that demonstrate your competency in the designated area(s).

You may find yourself in the position of needing to use a single critical incident in your experience to demonstrate two separate competencies on two separate KSAs. It is always better to use different incidents if possible, but sometimes that is not possible. If you have to use the same example in two different KSAs, you must rewrite the KSA to emphasize the different knowledge, skill, or ability you are addressing. It is very important to submit a different KSA response for each KSA prompt. Do not ever submit the same KSA response for two different KSA prompts within a single job application.

How Are KSAs Scored?

There are several ways KSA examiners can rate individual responses. They may use some variation on a point system or they may assign applications to one of several categories, from *Highly Qualified* to *Unqualified.*

The way for you to make sure your application ranks you near the top of the candidate pool is to address each KSA with the specifics that will make you stand out. It is not enough to simply say you supervised an office. You must present a narrative statement, written in the first person, describing how your duties as supervisor of an office qualifies you for the specific vacancy. You must use examples taken from your recent experience (within the past five years).

For example, a job announcement might specify that the successful applicant must be able to *negotiate with individuals and groups internally and externally.* Your task is to demonstrate, in a concise and to-the-point manner, that you have *already* successfully negotiated as required. What is important is to give examples of occasions you negotiated with groups and with individuals, both within an organization and externally to it. It is not important that the negotiations took place as part of a paid position.

Thinking about your life's experience, perhaps you realize that you served as president of a volunteer organization and you had to negotiate arrangements for a carnival fundraiser. In the course of organizing the carnival you had to find a way to reassure the owners and neighbors of last year's carnival site that the overflow crowds, noise, and litter of the previous fundraiser would be better managed this year. You also had to resolve a disagreement between two fellow volunteers about whose turn it was to supervise the booths. This is clearly a qualifying experience. You negotiated with both groups and individuals, and they were both within and external to your organization.

Your task is to write a first person account of your experience in such a way that it highlights the specific competencies mentioned in the vacancy announcement. The examiner will want to see the evidence that you possess the competencies required for the position. The best way to provide this evidence is to use the CCAR model for your response.

▶ CCAR GETS YOU WHERE YOU WANT TO GO

CCAR stands for Challenge, Context, Action, Results. The CCAR model for writing KSAs helps you address each competency in the most productive way. Working within this model enables you to maximize your education, experience, and training.

For example, perhaps you are interested in a career as an audiovisual producer. You go to OPM's website and discover that such careers are in the 1071 series. You search for open positions in the 1071 series and find several open positions, including one in your state that interests you. You read:

> Experience: You must have one year of specialized experience equivalent to the grade 07 level in the federal service. Specialized experience is work experience which required you to assist with the planning and production of video programs. You draft scripts; assist with the coordination of field productions, i.e., props, camera operation, and lighting and sound equipment; and assist in post-production, i.e., logging, editing, duplication, labeling and distribution of finished productions.
>
> EVALUATION CRITERIA—QUALITY RANKING FACTORS: Applicants meeting the minimum qualifications will be further evaluated based on the degree to which their experience, training, and education reflect possession of the following Quality Ranking Factors (QRFs).
>
> 1. Experience planning, developing, organizing, and directing the production of original video-taped training programs.
> 2. Experience working with outside contractors for specific activities related to the production of audiovisual training programs such as teleprompter operators, camera operators, sound technicians, and tape editors.
> 3. Knowledge of the components of an audio and video production system and the ability to use those components.

The essential experience is work, which may include unpaid work, assisting with the planning and production of video programs. The announcement then lists the many things you might do as a video production worker, from script preparation to post production. As you prepare to write, copy down the words used in the announcement (draft scripts, coordinate field production, props, camera operation, etc.) so that you can use them in your KSAs.

A KSA by Any Other Name

With very little practice, you will be able to identify KSAs by the many names they have in the federal job system. They could be Executive Core Qualifications, or Supplemental Statements, or Key Elements, or something else. No matter what they are called, the response you write should follow the CCAR model.

Even though the KSAs in this announcement are called Quality Ranking Factors (QRFs), they are KSAs as far as you are concerned. The first one is: Experience planning, developing, organizing, and directing the production of original videotaped training programs. That means you have to write a KSA (QRF) of a page to a page and a half about your experience producing video training programs.

Challenge

The first thing you want to do in each KSA is describe a specific challenge or problem you have faced in the course of your experience or education. In the case of the KSA/QRF about video training programs, you may have had an experience in which you were hired by Acme Window Shades to produce a training tape for their installers. The first thing you do in writing this KSA is set up the challenge. You might say something like: "I produced a thirty minute training video for Acme Window Shades. I had two weeks to research and write the script, hire the crew, shoot the video, and edit it."

Context

Next you want to talk about the setting of your challenge. First, ask yourself some questions. Who were the individuals and groups involved? What was the environment in which you worked? You have mentioned your time constraints, but were there also budgetary constraints? Did your cameraman get sick at the last minute, forcing you to shoot as well as direct? Was your supervisor on the project locked in a disagreement with her supervisor about the project, so that you were receiving conflicting input?

The context adds depth to the challenge. It personalizes the odds you overcame to triumph; and you *did* triumph, otherwise you would not be talking about it.

Action

Now you get to the core of your narrative, your mini-story. What actions did you take to meet the challenges you faced? How did you put together an informative and entertaining script while lining up crew and equipment? How did you eventually help your supervisor and her supervisor reach an agreement about the project? Be sure that you use the language from the Selective Factors section (remember *coordinate field production, props, camera operation*, and so on).

Results

This is perhaps the most important part of your KSA response, but many people seem to forget about it. Maybe it's because they do not want to seem to brag about themselves. Remember, you are being asked to talk about yourself, and you want to do it in a positive way. This is one time when you want to sound as confident as you possibly can. This exercise can be a good confidence builder for you. Most people do not focus on their successes as much as they criticize themselves for their failures. You may be overdue to think about your accomplishments.

In the case of the fictitious Acme Window Coverings video, how did you help your clients achieve their goals? What were they trying to accomplish, and how did your video production help them do it? Has the video been hailed by management and installers as an efficient and effective training tool? Did it win any awards? Furthermore, did you bring in the project on time and under budget? These are the kinds of questions you would ask yourself in that situation.

THE FIVE STEPS TO KSA SUCCESS

1. Brainstorm information about your life experiences.
2. Read the announcement's job description and KSA prompts carefully.
3. Analyze your experiences for KSA-related incidents and accomplishments.
4. Link your responses to the prompts by mirroring language from the vacancy announcement as you use the CCAR model.
5. Rewrite, polish, and proof your KSA responses.

What Are the Right Questions to Ask Yourself?

If you are not a video maker, you will have another set of questions that will apply to any given KSA. If you are an Information Technology worker, your KSA responses will address such things as specific computer program applications you have developed or software you have designed. What was your challenge; that is, why was a particular application or software needed? What was the context; what in the existing system needed improvement, and what obstacles stood in your way? What actions did you take? Did you initiate the development of the improvement or direct its implementation? What was the outcome? What additional efficiencies or capabilities resulted from your actions? Use specific supporting details such as man-hours or dollars saved.

If you are applying for a clerical or administrative job, one of the most common KSAs you will have to write must address your ability to communicate effectively, orally and in writing. Of course, by the very act of writing this KSA, you are demonstrating your ability to communicate effectively in writing; so make sure it is your very best effort. In deciding what to write about, you might want to mention two or three examples of your ability to communicate. Perhaps you were a standout on your high school debate team. If so, you might want to write about the time you faced the state champions (Challenge, Context) and won the debate (Action, Results). Maybe you have taught school or have been asked to train other employees in previous jobs. These are experiences that can demonstrate your ability to communicate orally. Again, be sure to address the results of your actions in specific terms, especially in terms of time and money.

Another common KSA will require you to address your interpersonal skills. To address this KSA, using the CCAR model, you must think of an interpersonal challenge you have faced: Disapproving supervisor who had to be won over? Prickly co-worker? Reluctant client? State the challenge, then expand on the context. What was the source of the problem (avoid placing blame)? Who else was involved? How did you analyze the nature of the problem and come up with a solution? What actions did you take, and how did your actions improve the situation (result)? Use details, particularly any improvements in productivity that resulted from your actions.

No matter what kind of KSA you are writing, it is vital that you use specific examples in your response. You may want to write the entire response about one example, if it is complex and revealing, or you may want to use up to three examples in a single response. The important thing is to use lots of details and specifics about your example, while avoiding any work-related jargon or acronyms. You are telling a short story to the examiner. Do not be afraid to personalize your response; the examiners are human, and like all humans, they will enjoy a good story. The more appealing you are to the examiner, the more likely you are to wind up near the top of the list of candidates.

Your Application Represents You

In the remaining chapters of this book you will learn how to write exceptional KSAs. It is vitally important that your KSAs be exceptional. There are many applicants for federal jobs, and only the top three applicants are typically interviewed. Until you get to that personal interview, the application is all the examiners can know about you.

Your KSAs in particular must be flawless. Make sure there are no spelling mistakes. Proofread each KSA several times. Read it aloud; and then have someone else read it aloud to you, so that you will know how it sounds to other people. Think of your KSAs as sample work products. If there are any mistakes in your KSAs, your potential supervisor will assume your work also goes out with mistakes in it.

▶ SUMMARY

This chapter has not only introduced you to the concept of KSAs, but also to the model for writing them. Using the tips in this chapter, including defining your challenge, context, action, and results, you will be prepared to write a KSA that will help you get the job you want. Remember, asking yourself questions about your knowledge, skills, and abilities will prepare you to start writing. Keep reading for information about preparing to write.

5

Preparing to Write

You are looking to embark on an exciting journey with all the dynamic opportunities that federal jobs provide. However, you are also competing with some of the best candidates around. How do you show your special worth to the reading team who will be rating and ranking your application package? By submitting excellent KSA responses. Consider these crucial steps:

1. Approach the job announcement carefully, acquainting yourself with what experience and qualities the federal agency is looking for.

2. Evaluate your resume to ensure that it is complete, including **all** required information.

3. Read and think about the three to six criteria (KSA requirements) given for each vacancy announcement.

4. Prewrite, outline, write, and edit each KSA response. Your challenge is to capture in writing how your experiences match the knowledge, skills, and abilities required for the specific job.

The following chapters address Steps 3 and 4, guiding you in creating your best possible KSA responses. In this chapter, the focus is preparing to write: writing with your reader in mind, prewriting, and outlining.

HELPFUL HINT—GIVE THEM WHAT THEY WANT

KSAs can work to your advantage. By studying the job description and the KSA requirements, you can craft responses that mirror back to the hiring officials the very traits and talents that they have defined as essential to the job.

▶ PREWRITING

Why do you have to write KSA responses? Basically, you are enhancing your concise federal resume with additional context. In responding to the 3–6 KSA requirements in a job announcement, you have the opportunity to tell your unique story, giving detailed examples of the challenges and goals you have met in particular situations. Let's start with prewriting.

Prewriting consists of these tasks:

▶ considering your audience
▶ understanding each KSA requirement
▶ brainstorming which contexts, challenges, actions, and results to use
▶ jotting down notes or sketching a diagram (if that helps you organize your thoughts)

Spend time on prewriting. It's probably the least appreciated element to effective writing. Some authors prewrite, or brainstorm, entirely in their heads; others toss ideas around with friends; while others jot down ideas or sketch webs or diagrams. There is no right way to approach prewriting.

Consider Your Audience

Writing should always be audience-specific. In any communication, *what* you say and *how* you say it depends entirely on *to whom* you are saying it. This means that before you begin to write, you need to know your audience. The more you know about your readers, the better you will be able to write for them. That includes anticipating your audience's needs and expectations and tailoring your KSA response appropriately.

The first step in prewriting, then, is to think about your readers, your audience. Start by considering the answers to these five questions:

1. Who will read my application package?
2. Why are they reading it?
3. What is my goal?
4. What is my message to my audience?
5. What special needs or characteristics does this group of readers have?

Let's quickly analyze these questions one at a time.

1. Who will read my application package?

Who is your audience? It helps to keep in mind the people who will read, rate, and rank your application package. Depending on the federal agency involved and the level of the job opening, your readers will most certainly include people with some rather impressive job titles:

- ▶ human resource manager
- ▶ personnel staffing specialist
- ▶ Rating and selecting official
- ▶ hiring manager or hiring panel
- ▶ executive resource staff
- ▶ subject matter expert (SME)
- ▶ Qualifications Review Board (QRB)

2. Why are they reading it?

Your readers review dozens—maybe hundreds—of KSA responses. They *want* to discover the standouts. They want to see specific examples that are appropriate, concise, and interesting. If your KSA responses are well written, the reader will not have to look back through your resume to see if you have the experiences that relate to the skills they need.

The first reader verifies that you have *thoroughly* completed your application package and met the basic requirements for federal employment. (Many applicants don't make it past this point.) Subsequent reader(s) determine if you meet the announcement's qualifications and are QUALIFIED or HIGHLY QUALIFIED. At this point, readers review your KSA responses (graded from 5 to 20 points). They rank and rate your application and build a Best Qualified Candidates List. When your name reaches this list, your application moves forward to the hiring manager or hiring panel for consideration—or, if your job is technical or scientific, to the subject matter expert.

3. What is my goal?

Your goal in writing excellent KSA responses is simple: **Convince your audience that you are the best candidate by tying your experiences and training to the qualifications of the job you want**. You need to tell the reader you are expert, proficient, highly qualified, or skilled at certain things. To accomplish this goal, you will fashion a succinct first-person narrative of 2/3 to 1-1/2 pages for each KSA requirement. Thoughtful KSA responses, along with a strong resume, will get you the interview you need to land the federal job you aspire to.

4. What is my message to my audience?

Your primary underlying message is "I am the best person for this position." Your examples and details should *always* support this message. A secondary message might be "I am flexible, cooperative, resourceful, open-minded, enthusiastic, trustworthy, and talented or experienced (or both)."

Moreover, if you are attracted to a job that you do not match perfectly, federal hiring managers suggest "Apply anyway." In this case, your underlying message is "I can adapt my experiences and personal characteristics to handle the job's requirements—and do even better than someone who matches perfectly."

5. What special needs does this group of readers have?

One thing your readers probably need is more time. Don't waste a reader's time with unnecessary embellishment or stale, trite language. Also, your readers need to fill one or more positions; they want an application package that is complete, clear, appropriate, and interesting. They need you to *read all the directions* and *follow them*. For example, some hiring personnel will not read an application that is written in pencil when black pen was specified. Remember, these reviewers will evaluate many applications for your posting. They are searching for compelling evidence that you are the one. Maybe saying that your readers want to be "dazzled" is going too far—but they *do* want to pick the best candidate who stands out from the crowd.

In accordance, you will want to paint an impressive (but honest) picture in the readers' minds, detailing the size and scope of your accomplishments. To illustrate, can you mark the difference between "I ran a Peace Corps community event" and "I envisioned and coordinated an annual state-wide Peace Corps festival with 60 participants and 1,800 visitors"?

HELPFUL HINT—MIND READERS? NOT THESE READERS!

Do not assume that your readers will pull needed KSA information out of your application package, picking up the important points. *They will not.* Even if there were time for such insight, reviewers are not allowed to infer anything. So spell out your experiences in clear language.

What KSA Readers Want From You

Let's discuss what KSA readers want from you, the job candidate:

- ▶ completeness
- ▶ specifics
- ▶ conciseness
- ▶ adaptability

Completeness. You need to consider that this is the federal government: If you want to beat out your competition, complete all paperwork and follow all directions. Federal job applications are designed to eliminate favoritism and provide a level playing field by using the same paperwork requirements, selective factors, and quality ranking factors for all applicants. If you can keep this in mind when completing your application, your chances of landing the job will be greatly enhanced. Finally, make sure that you follow any recommended format or instructions on the job announcement.

Specifics. Federal human resource managers get tired of reading generic statements that don't say anything different than the applicant's resume. So now many vacancy announcements specifically say: "Generic responses to KSAs will not be accepted." Hiring officials can get the generic information from your resume, and generic or general information is not helpful information. What they want and need are the specifics.

Therefore, use dates, dollar amounts, percentages, man-hours, and volume to detail your accomplishments. How much time/money did your suggestions save your company? What's the number of contracts you handled per week? How exactly did you improve your office or work environment?

DETAILS!

Qualify means to modify or restrict. In this sentence, words that qualify are in *italics*: I served as the *first high-ranking* officer in the *Navy's unique research* team.

Quantify means to express in numbers or measurement elements such as when, how much, how many, how often, and what scope. In this sentence, words that quantify are in *italics*: *Twice per year* during the *four-day* EPA conferences in *1999–2002,* I planned and cooked *three* meals a day for *more than 50* attendees.

Conciseness. Conciseness means being succinct, brief, to-the-point, and not rambling on. A sure way to annoy your reader is to state an idea or piece of information more than once within your KSAs. Writers repeat themselves unnecessarily because they are not sure that they have been clear or they are not attentive to the need to be concise.

Further, a proactive vocabulary—especially, powerful verbs—can often repair wordiness (and certainly make your story more interesting to read). An example: "I conceived of *and* directed *the study*" *is more concise than* "I took some time to think about, plan, and lead *the study.*" Proactive vocabulary should be both compelling and precise. (Find proactive vocabulary lists in Chapter 6.)

Adaptability. Hiring staff expect you to *adapt* your knowledge, skills, and abilities to meet broadly similar, yet specific, requirements of a prospective job. In other words, translate your strengths. Many jobs share skills. For instance, it's not only a social worker who must possess "the ability to identify and obtain resources or services needed to assist others." Nor is it only a customer service representative who needs "skill in written and oral communication." Workers in many occupations need to show an ability "to work with management officials to develop policy and guidelines."

If you are seeking a career change, you can adapt your experiences into equivalent skills, by using the vocabulary of the field you are interested in. For example, applicant Margaret wants to win an Assistant Library Technician job. She is coming from a U.S. Army supply clerk position. She researches keywords on the Internet and then adapts her resume and KSA responses to reflect the language of librarians (set here in *italics*):

In my latest position as Supply Clerk at the 34th General Hospital in Munich, Germany, I maintained a complete *library* of forms. This included seeing that every blank form used throughout the hospital system was *catalogued* and *filed* (over 700 different forms). I devised an up-to-date *inventory*. In addition, I *processed* and *catalogued* new *materials* (*books*, *videotapes*, and *CDs*) into the hospital *library*.

Understand Each KSA Requirement

Before you begin brainstorming what to write, **read each specific KSA requirement carefully**. Print it on the top of your paper. Be sure you understand what the requirement means. If you do not understand it, call or e-mail the federal agency as indicated in the job announcement.

Study these sample KSA requirements, each followed by a sample job. The KSA tends to be written in general terms, even within a specific field. Be aware that several generic requirements, such as **"Ability to communicate orally and in writing,"** are found repeatedly throughout the range of federal jobs that are described in Chapter 1.

KSA Requirement	Sample Job
Ability to communicate orally and in writing.	Contract Administrator
Ability to operate engineering equipment safely.	Engineering Equipment Operator
Skill in practicing good customer service.	Editorial Assistant
Ability to lead or supervise.	Intelligence Operations Supervisor
Knowledge of medical terminology.	Health Technician
Ability to work independently for extended periods.	Criminal Investigator
Skill in coordinating and working with individuals and groups to accomplish work objectives and assignments.	Insurance Management Specialist
Ability to interpret instructions and specifications.	Cook Supervisor
Skill in applying both conventional and innovative fact-finding, analytical, and problem-solving methods and techniques to analyze facts, identify problems, report findings, and make conclusions, to include what appropriate and corrective action was taken.	Equal Opportunity Advisor

Ready, Set, Brainstorm

You can now search for experiences and challenges in your life that relate to the individual KSA requirements. **Brainstorming** entails thinking, remembering, and trying out ideas without being critical. Your job is to **consider one KSA requirement and how it is exemplified in your life story**: schooling, past jobs, awards, challenges, training, emergencies, volunteering. Some prefer to think over which elements to include and later put pen to paper. Some might scribble notes as they think. Others draw webs or trees or maps, some take random notes, some make lists, some outline. Your resume can help spark ideas or it might hinder you at this point. There is no one right way.

HELPFUL HINT—PREWRITING RULE OF THUMB

Logic and organization aren't important in prewriting. The goal is to be thorough. Explore your examples on paper, toss out ideas, identify points to be made, add supporting detail.

Let's say the KSA requirement you are writing about is the ability to lead or supervise. Think of all the times you used leadership skills, especially in a challenging environment. Here are some examples you might write down.

Examples

Organizing a food co-operative among the tenants of your apartment building; serving as co-chair of a fund raising activity when your temple's operating budget falls short; explaining work flow procedures to new members of your staff while keeping it fresh and interesting to your coworkers.

You might jot these leadership examples down randomly on paper and then label them from *most responsibility required* to *least responsibility required*, or *most interesting challenge* to *least interesting challenge*.

When brainstorming, don't forget to consider all of the following elements of your life story before selecting the best, most pertinent ones:

- ▶ undergraduate and graduate schooling
- ▶ degrees, additional training, and certifications
- ▶ part-time and full-time jobs
- ▶ workshops and seminars
- ▶ volunteer positions
- ▶ emergencies, family crises
- ▶ awards and commendations
- ▶ quotes from satisfied customers, clients, and supervisors
- ▶ team projects
- ▶ professional, physical, and emotional goals
- ▶ professional, physical, and emotional challenges

HELPFUL HINT—COMMUNITY SERVICE COUNTS

Community service and volunteer work are relevant and add to your "likeability" factor. If you are a Girl Scout leader or a trustee for a co-op association, use it in your KSA responses. These examples might well fit KSA qualities such as the ability to lead or supervise or the ability to plan and coordinate.

Let CCAR Drive Your Brainstorming, Outlining, and KSA Responses

Before reviewing the CCAR model presented in Chapter 4, let's make one thing clear: You should try to be comfortable brainstorming and reviewing during prewriting and outlining. Adapting and refining ideas is exactly what the eraser and the delete key are for.

As you learned in Chapter 4, the Office of Personnel Management (OPM) has designed and recommends the CCAR model for writing KSA responses or Executive Core Qualifications (ECQs), in the case of Senior Executive Service positions.

Recall that **CCAR** stands for **C**ontext, **C**hallenge, **A**ction and **R**esults. You may mix these elements or present them in a different order. To review:

▶ **Context:** The setting. The factors that contributed to a challenge you faced, such as budget limits, staffing changes, or institutional reform; the clients, customers, colleagues, supervisors, and groups you worked with; the environment in which you worked to tackle a particular challenge (members of Congress, unhappy clients, low morale, a move to a new office).

▶ **Challenge:** The specific problem or goal you had to address.

▶ **Action:** The steps you chose to solve the problem. The specific actions you took to address a challenge or reach a goal.

▶ **Results:** The outcome—the difference that you made. Detailed examples of the results of your actions, proving the quality and effectiveness of your skills.

How to Pick Examples

Your readers want examples that demonstrate how you met challenges and achieved goals. For example, the ability to communicate orally: You are a framing store manager and you communicate with your employees, your customers, and your suppliers. You probably talk to people in meetings and in person to help them sell products, complete framing jobs, restock the store, and meet deadlines. Think of a challenge or goal where your skill at communicating orally had positive outcomes. (e.g., Due to a mix-up in framing orders, you had a very unhappy customer. You apologized, explaining how you would rectify the problem, won back the customer with compensation and extra service, resulting in her loyalty—and in her bringing more customers to your store.)

Remember, **your KSA responses should be very results oriented**. In other words, choose compelling experiences with positive outcomes.

GO FOR IT

Try reviewing your experiences in order—from ten years ago to the present—so as not to skip a good example. Remember, experiences you had in one job, or how you handled one crisis, may translate to match the particular KSA quality you are addressing. Moreover, the qualities and skills you have most likely apply to more than one KSA (e.g., you have excellent oral communications skills, which apply to both the ability to meet and deal with the general public and the ability to interpret and communicate instructions and specifications).

Ten questions to ask yourself that may trigger memories to choose experiences from:

1. What jobs or volunteer positions have I had that are unusual?
2. Which goals and challenges am I proud to have met?
3. What family, social, or travel experiences have I had that were very challenging?
4. What kind of skills and knowledge do I use in my work?

5. How complex is my current or past job?
6. What guidelines do I use to accomplish my work?
7. How much judgment do I have to exercise on the job?
8. What kind of supervision do I give?
9. What kind of supervision do I receive?
10. Who do I have contact with and what is my role?

HELPFUL HINT—THE RIGHT EXAMPLE

To demonstrate a KSA quality, choose recent examples, within the last five to eight years. Select one vivid example or two lesser (or related) examples for each KSA. The number of examples is not as important as assuring that your experience matches the KSA requirements. Try to use separate examples for each KSA, but if the example is significant, you might emphasize different skills or qualities within the same experience. Choose examples from both paid and volunteer experiences.

▶ OUTLINING IN THE CCAR MODEL

Good writing begins with organization. Webbing, diagramming, note-taking, and outlining—are all viable methods to organize your thoughts on paper. Here are some outlines. The first outline format is for two examples, each with one context, action, and one or more results. The second outline format shows one impressive experience with two challenges, each having separate actions and results. As you can imagine, there are many variations of the elements called Context, Challenge, Action, and Results.

The following guided outline showcases two examples for one KSA requirement. Even though you may eventually mix up the elements of the CCAR model, for now, follow this order of headings. Fill in the spaces with two examples that fit the specific KSA requirement:

KSA = _____

I. One Example

    A. Context [setting (your title, dates, location), others involved, contributing circumstances]

    B. Challenge or Goal [What was the challenge or goal you addressed?]

    C. Action [What steps did you take? What specific actions?]

    D. Results [What happened? What were the outcomes? Quantify and qualify.]

II. Another Example

    A. Context [setting (your title, dates, location), others involved, contributing circumstances]

    B. Challenge or Goal [What was the challenge or goal you addressed?]

    C. Action [What steps did you take? What specific actions?]

    D. Results [What happened? What were the outcomes? Quantify and qualify.]

The following example of an outline filled in with notes becomes a rough draft of a KSA response on page 118 in Chapter 8.

KSA = Ability to work and cooperate with others, interact tactfully, and be responsive to a culturally diverse workplace.

I. [Example] Chester Brown and his negative attitude

    A. [Context] acting supervisor, Lake Ave St., Altadena; 2 months; veteran employee bitter, angry; disliked management; coworkers dislike him

    B. [Challenge or Goal] turn Chester around; bring out his positives; help coworkers appreciate him; encourage working together in diversity

    C. [Action] encouraged respect for him; join us for breakfast, asked him questions; involved in daily operations; Safety Captain thing; wrote complaint letter to telephone company for him

    D. [Results] Chester was happier; contributed to team; others began to respect him, invited to breakfast; became more open to him; I communicate/cooperate with others and motivate coworkers to do same; I am tactful, I could find his skills (safety, experience), accept diversity (cranky, older employee)

Another possible outline showcases one example with more than one challenge:

KSA = _____

I. One Example's Context [setting (your title, dates, location), others involved, contributing circumstances]

II. First Challenge or Goal [What was the challenge or goal you addressed?]

    A. Action [What steps did you take? What specific actions?]

    B. Results [What happened? What were the outcomes? Quantify and qualify.]

III. Second Challenge or Goal [What was the challenge or goal you addressed?]

    A. Action [What steps did you take? What specific actions?]

    B. Results [What happened? What were the outcomes? Quantify and qualify.]

Now it's your turn. Imagine you are writing a response for the **Ability to communicate effectively in writing**:

KSA = _____

A. Context [setting (your title, dates, location), others involved, contributing circumstances]

_____

_____

_____

_____

B. Challenge or Goal [What was the challenge or goal you addressed?]

_____

_____

_____

_____

_____

C. Action [What steps did you take? What specific actions?]

_____

_____

_____

_____

D. Results [What happened? What were the outcomes? Quantify and qualify.]

_____

_____

_____

_____

_____

▶ HOW TO OUTLINE YOUR ENDING

Unlike most types of communication—reports, letters, stories—your KSA responses do *not* have a conclusion. The most common and effective ending for your KSA is to list your education, training, and awards. Some of these items you may be pulling from your resume; others may have been inappropriate for your resume, but perfectly appropriate here (e.g., a workshop in conflict resolution or an employee-of-the-month award).

First, choose a boldface heading such as:

Education and Training
Highlights of Education and Training Related to This KSA
Overview of Skills and Knowledge
My Education and Awards Related to This KSA Include

Next, list all relevant degrees, workshops, seminars, training, certifications, awards, and commendations.

Here are two examples of such endings, one with a bulleted list and the second with a short one-sentence introduction followed by a list:

Education and Training Related to This KSA
▶ Master of Science, Computer Science, Yale University (2003)
▶ Racine Award for Excellence (2001)
▶ Peter Norton Computer Programming and Language seminars (2000)

▶ Bachelor of Science degree, Computer Science, University of California at Santa Cruz; graduated Magna Cum Laude (1999)

Additional Training Related to This KSA:

In addition to holding an A.A. from the DeLuis Agriculture and Technical School, I believe the following education and training have enhanced my knowledge in the area of these KSAs:

2003, Management Change in the Workplace (seminar)
2000, Creative Problem Solving (workshops I and II)
1998, Conflict Resolution
1997, Community CPR (adult, child, and infant)

▶ SUMMARY

Remember your audience and the characteristics they look for in a KSA response before you ever put pen to paper. Carefully read the KSA requirement you are addressing, then brainstorm relevant experiences from your experiences and training. Next translate your notes or diagram into an outline using the CCAR model. Luckily for you, the use of KSAs in federal vacancy announcements represents an excellent opportunity to match yourself to a job's requirements and to increase your chances of being hired.

6 Choosing the Right Words

The goal of the KSA statement is to tie your experiences to the qualifications needed for a specific job as clearly and succinctly as you can. Choosing potent, exact wording set in a professional tone will showcase your knowledge, skills, and abilities—and separate you from the pack. In Chapter 5 we discussed writing with your reader in mind, outlining, and prewriting. In this chapter, we analyze how to use words wisely.

The key to a good KSA statement is getting the right information to your audience in a fast, readable style. How do you do this? By using the minimum words for the maximum impact. However, you *do* want to include enough detail and powerful language to give yourself credit for your accomplishments. Consider the following examples:

Version 1: Worked in an office for a few years.

This example says almost nothing. The next version includes more helpful information:

Version 2: Provided administrative support from 1999-2003 for a law firm.

This is better, but is it very impressive? Not really. Now read version 3.

Version 3: Provided administrative support for six litigation lawyers at the firm of Frank and Cauley. Managed the court appearance schedules of each, coordinated staff meetings, and recorded the highlights of said meetings. Responsible for tracking incoming and outgoing correspondence, and for maintaining inventory of office supplies. Coordinated travel schedules and expense reports when necessary. Implemented training program for new administrative assistants.

Now what do you think? All three versions are describing the same job. Version 1, although true, does little to explain the experience. Version 2 includes more detail, but would you hire someone who could summarize their experience and skills in one sentence? Version 3 includes details and strong language to describe the same job.

The good news is that it is not hard to learn how to highlight your talents and experiences. You can showcase your own knowledge, skills, and abilities in excellent KSA statements by following a few simple writing guidelines.

- ▶ Use appropriate formality.
- ▶ Be active, not passive.
- ▶ Choose a proactive vocabulary.
- ▶ Understand denotation and connotation.
- ▶ Convey a positive tone.
- ▶ Keep it brief and clear.

Remember, the more you practice these guidelines, the better you will become.

▶ USE APPROPRIATE FORMALITY

As a rule, the level of formality in your writing should increase when your audience is of a higher rank, or is less familiar to you. It is true that your KSA statement is written in the first person (*I, me, my, myself*), which is commonly considered a personal and informal mode of narration. However, in all other aspects, your KSA writing should reflect the degree of formality you use when addressing a prospective employer—not a friend or colleague. You will want to avoid informal, casual word usage, or **colloquialisms**, such as:

- ▶ contractions
- ▶ slang
- ▶ archaic or pretentious words
- ▶ clichés
- ▶ vulgarisms—obscene or offensive language

Avoid Contractions

The use of **contractions** (*I'm, could've, wouldn't*) is common in speech; in fact, it sounds stilted if you avoid them. However, in KSA writing, use full words rather than contractions:

> *NO:* **It's** also my job to regulate the import of cargo.
>
> *YES:* **It is** also my job to regulate the import of cargo.

> *NO:* Among my duties as a Canine Enforcement Officer, **I've** trained three drug detector dogs.
>
> *YES:* Among my duties as a Canine Enforcement Officer, **I have** trained three drug detector dogs.

Avoid Slang

Slang is non-standard English. It does not belong in KSA writing. Its significance is typically far removed from either its denotative or connotative meaning (see page 75), and slang is often particular to a certain group (therefore, possibly excluding your readers). Examples include: *canned, blow off, no sweat,* and *chill.*

> *NO:* My supervisor gave me a **thumbs up** on my Food Services Management project.
>
> *YES:* My supervisor **approved** my Food Services Management project.

Avoid Archaic or Pretentious Words

As with all business writing, avoid the use of archaic and pretentious terms in your KSA statement. **Archaic** words and phrases are old-fashioned, although still found in poetry, plays, and literature. Examples are *twain* (two), *afore* (before), *thou* (you), and *hither and yon* (here and there). **Pretentious** words and phrases sound affected and overblown, such as *ascertain* in place of *determine*, or *cogitate* in place of *think about*. Note: This guideline does *not* mean "Don't use adult words or long words"—just try to use the clearest and most succinct words.

> *NO:* **As per** my supervisor, I analyzed the conflict quickly.
>
> *YES:* **According to** my supervisor, I analyzed the conflict quickly.

Avoid Clichés

Clichés, or trite expressions, should be avoided—not only because they are informal and overused, but also because it will seem like you lack originality for using them. Your writing should project your own voice without relying on stale phrases such as: *add insult to injury, cream of the crop, grin and bear it,* and *pay the piper.*

> *NO:* In May, 2001, I left that **rat race** to become a contract specialist.
>
> *YES:* In May, 2001, I left that **position at Pallay and Sons** to become a contract specialist.

HELPFUL HINT—PROPER TITLES

Write out full names and exact courtesy titles (Mr.; Ms.; Dr.; Professor; the CEO; Ms. Jane Smythe, Esquire) when you refer to others:

NO: My examining officers, **Racine** and **Hannah Schiffman**, awarded me two certificates of excellence between June and October, 2003.

YES: My examining officers, **Mr.** Ned Racine and **Dr.** Hannah Schiffman, awarded me two certificates of excellence between June and October, 2003.

Avoid Vulgarisms

Vulgarisms are obscene or offensive language. Obviously, you do not want to offend or degrade your readers. Swearing and obscene language have no place in job hunting.

Additionally, always avoid bias in your writing, including negative stereotypes or degrading others. Replace any possibly offensive words and phrases with *inclusive language*.

▶ BE ACTIVE, NOT PASSIVE

Good writers are intentional. Read the following sentence.

> *The bedroom doorknob was turned slowly, squeaky on its spindle.*

The author of the sentence above intentionally chose the passive voice, so the reader does not know who is turning that squeaky doorknob. Betsy turned the squeaky bedroom doorknob slowly (active voice) just does not have the same suspenseful feel to it, does it? If you are not writing a mystery, however, try to avoid passive voice, in favor of active voice. Why, you may ask? Well, let's compare these two KSA sentences:

PASSIVE VOICE: The EEO policies and procedures were compiled and implemented within two months. (Who *compiled and implemented them? The passive voice as used here is vague, annoying, and awkward.*)

ACTIVE VOICE: I compiled the EEO policies and procedures and oversaw their implementation within two months. (*The active voice answers "who," while conveying energy and directness.*)

As you can see, the **active voice** is simple and direct, one of the major goals of KSA writing. It connects an action with the person who is performing that action. The **passive voice** renders

SAY NO TO BIAS!

Gender

- Avoid the suffix *–ess,* which has the effect of minimizing the significance of the word to which it is attached (*actor* is preferable to *actress, proprietor* to *proprietress*).
- Do not overuse *he, his,* and *him* when writing in general terms. For example, choose *he or she* or alternate between *he* and *she,* or use a title instead (*the manager*).
- De-gender occupations. *Businessman* becomes *businessperson* or *executive, chairman* becomes *chair* or *chairperson, stewardess* becomes *flight attendant, weatherman* becomes *meteorologist.*
- Use professional, rather than personal, descriptive terms. *Inappropriate*: Karen Healy, a lovely associate. *Appropriate*: Karen Healy, an experienced associate.

Race

- To avoid stereotyping, leave out any reference to race, unless it is relevant to your KSAs, such as describing the report on racial diversity you created for your company.
- As in any business writing, focus on a person's individual, professional characteristics and qualifications, not racial characteristics.

Disability

- Always put the person ahead of the disability, as in *person with impaired hearing*, rather than *hearing-impaired person*.
- If your writing is specifically focused on disabilities or disease (for example, you were an Army nurse), do not use words that imply victimization or create negative stereotypes. Terms such as *victim, sufferer, poor, afflicted*, and *unfortunate* should be omitted.

the *doer* of the action less obvious, if that person is ever identified at all. Moreover, sentences written in the passive voice tend to be longer and more difficult to understand. They seem to lack focus. The active voice, however, feels concise and focused.

Remember, when you write in the active voice, the subject of the sentence causes, or is the source of, the action. In the passive voice, the subject is acted upon. Compare two more sets of examples:

PASSIVE VOICE: *It was suggested by me that my staff provide a written report.*
ACTIVE VOICE: *I suggested that my staff provide a written report.*

PASSIVE VOICE: *A phone conference was scheduled for Thursday mornings.*
ACTIVE VOICE: *My team scheduled a phone conference for Thursday mornings.*

PASSIVE VOICE: *Three finalists for the open position had been selected by the human resources team.*

ACTIVE VOICE: *The human resources team had selected three finalists for the open position.*

Finally, the passive voice can sound "sneaky," since people might use it to avoid taking the blame for something. How many times have you heard, "Mistakes were made" or "It is regrettable that . . . ?" The passive voice allows the speaker to apologize without really apologizing.

HELPFUL HINT—TURNING PASSIVE INTO ACTIVE

Sometimes the best way to understand a writing guideline is to play with it and practice what you have read. Using a separate sheet of paper, try making these passive sentences more direct.

1. It was decided by the director of human services that the old filing system would be revived.
2. The Employee of the Month is the award that was won by me.
3. The local light-rail train was the method of transportation chosen.

▶ CHOOSE A PROACTIVE VOCABULARY

Whether writing a resume or a KSA statement, you will want to impress the selecting official with your independence, energy, and initiative. One of your basic tools for this goal is a proactive vocabulary. What follows are descriptions of elements of the CCAR model, including lists of powerful, proactive words. They can be very useful when you are stuck for a word or you find yourself repeating yourself. Of course, these words can be modified as needed.

Challenge
Describe a specific problem or challenge: *challenge, difficulty, dilemma, goal, impediment, issue, obstacle, problem, project, shrinking budget, low morale.*

Context
Give specific details on individuals, groups, clients, colleagues, co-workers, members of Congress; specify the environment you worked in, dates, and places.

Action
Discuss the specific actions you took and the creativity you used: *action, address (a challenge), assemble, author, conceive, convene, create, design, deploy, draft, edit, employ, exercise, forge, form, formulate, generate, highlight, implement, initiate, invent, negotiate, plan, publish, showcase, spearhead, use, utilize.*

Demonstrate leadership: *administrator, chief of, control over, decide, direct, execute, foreman, govern, head up, in charge of, lead, manage, manager, oversee, responsible for, run, staff, supervise, supervisor, team leader.*

Describe teamwork and persuasion skills: *coach, convince, counsel, galvanize, inspire, invigorate, lobby, persuade, rally, restore, unify, unite, revitalize.*

Result

Give examples of specific result of your actions: *accomplish, accomplishment, achieve, attain, communication, conclusion, cooperation, cost-effective, efficiency, leadership, master, morale, outcome, output, productivity, solution, succeed, success, sustain.*

Demonstrate your competencies: *able, adept, capable, competent, demonstrate, detail-oriented, excellence, highly effective, expert, fully, good, great, high-quality, knowledgeable, outstanding, powerful, proven, quality, seasoned, significantly, skilled, special, superb, tested, trained, tried, versed in.*

If you are naturally modest, you need to put that modesty aside for a while. Be honest, but accentuate your strengths. If you do not tell your readers you were the only safety control officer for 24 people, how will they know? Use qualifiers such as

chief	key	single
expert	lead	singular
first	leading	sole
first-class	major	source
foremost	most	top
greatest	only	unique
guiding	primary	unparalleled
head	prime	unrivaled
high-ranking	principal	

Frequency and Scope

It is essential to qualify your KSAs with *when, how often*, and *how long* your jobs, projects, and tasks lasted. The Navy Job Kit instructions recommend that choosing modifiers to define the frequency at which you perform tasks: *occasionally, regularly, annually, once or twice per year, weekly, monthly, yearly, daily, every morning at 10:00 A.M.* Finally, try to use words that define the level and scope of your experience and skills, such as *first-ever, novel, wide-ranging, sole, longest, universal, foremost.*

FREQUENTLY USED ACTION WORDS FOR KSA STATEMENTS

One government website, http://ohrm.cc.nih.gov/employ/KSAs/KSAwords.htm, provides this list of past-tense verbs to use in resumes and KSAs. Some are mentioned before, but they are worth repeating.

A

accomplished
achieved
acquired
acted
adapted
added
adjusted
administered
advanced
allocated
allotted
allowed
analyzed
anticipated
applied
appointed
appraised
arbitrated
arranged
assessed
assigned
assisted
assured
attained
audited
authorized
awarded

B

based
bought
briefed

budgeted
built

C

catalogued
calculated
caused
centralized
certified
chaired
changed
clarified
classified
closed
collaborated
collected
combined
commended
communicated
compared
competed
compiled
completed
composed
computed
conceived
conceptualized
concluded
conducted
conferred
confirmed
considered
consolidated

constructed
consulted
continued
contracted
controlled
convened
converted
conveyed
convinced
cooperated
coordinated
corrected
correlated
counseled
created
critiqued
cultivated

D

dealt
debated
decided
defended
defined
delegated
delivered
demonstrated
described
designated
designed
developed
devised
diagnosed

directed
discovered
disseminated
distributed
documented
drafted
duplicated

E
earned
edited
educated
eliminated
employed
enabled
encouraged
endorsed
enforced
engineered
enlarged
enlisted
ensured
equipped
established
estimated
evaluated
exercised
experimented
explained

F
facilitated
filed
financed
finished
focused
forecasted
formed
formulated

fostered
founded
fulfilled

G
gathered
generated
graded
granted
guided

H
handled
helped
hired
hosted

I
identified
illustrated
implemented
improved
incorporated
indexed
indicated
informed
influenced
initiated
innovated
inspected
installed
instructed
insured
integrated
interacted
interpreted
interviewed
introduced
invested

investigated
involved
issued

J
judged
justified

L
launched
lead
lectured
linked
located
logged

M
maintained
managed
mandated
marketed
measured
mediated
minimized
modified
monitored
motivated

N
negotiated
notified
nullified

O
observed
obtained
opened
operated
ordered

originated
organized
outlined
oversaw

P
participated
performed
persuaded
pioneered
planned
prepared
predicted
presented
prevented
priced
printed
processed
procured
produced
programmed
projected
promoted
proposed
protected
provided
publicized
published
purchased
pursued

Q
quantified
questioned

R
ranked
rated

recognized
recommended
reconciled
recruited
reduced
referred
regulated
rejected
released
reorganized
replaced
replied
reported
represented
requested
required
researched
resolved
responded
reevaluated
reviewed
revised
rewarded

S
scheduled
screened
selected
separated
serviced
set up
settled
simplified
simulated
solicited
solved
sorted
specified

staffed
structured
studied
submitted
substituted
succeeded
suggested
summarized
supervised
surveyed
synthesized

T
tabulated
targeted
taught
tested
testified
trained
transcribed
transferred
translated
transmitted
triggered
turned

U
updated
upgraded
utilized

V
validated
volunteered

W
weighed
wrote

▶ UNDERSTAND DENOTATION AND CONNOTATION

When writing your KSA statement, keep in mind that you probably have only one chance to win over your readers. They are busy people and can't be bothered spending time trying to figure out what you mean. But you can do it! You already have a command of the English language that includes knowledge of thousands of words' **denotative** (literal or primary) meanings. Therefore, it is easy to choose the right ones to get your message across, right?

Well, not necessarily! The challenge comes when a word has not just a *denotative* meaning, but also a *connotative* meaning. **Connotation** is a word's implied meaning, which involves emotions, cultural assumptions, and suggestions. Connotative meanings can be positive, negative, or neutral. You should consider both denotation and connotation when making word choices.

For example, what ideas come to mind when you hear the word *skinny*? Thin? *Skinny* has negative connotations, while *thin* is a more neutral selection. What are the connotative differences between *copy* and *plagiarize*? Between *leer* and *look*?

If you were writing about a business retreat where, during a workshop you directed, executives played favorite childhood games, you would not choose the adjective *childish* to describe their behavior. *Childish* has a connotative meaning of immaturity, whereas *childlike*, a better choice, does not.

Similarly, in describing a past job in a county social worker's office, you should realize that the words *vagrant* and *homeless* have the same denotative meaning, but that *vagrant* connotes a public nuisance, whereas *homeless* suggests an unfortunate situation worthy of attention and assistance.

Some dictionaries offer usage notes that help explain connotative meanings, but the best thing to rely upon is your own experience and the experience of the friends and family members who read your KSA drafts.

▶ CONVEY A POSITIVE TONE

Your reading audience will form an opinion of you based on a number of factors in your KSA statements. The tone you use is vitally important. **Tone** refers to the attitude you show both to your reader and about your subject. It can be respectful or cocky, optimistic or pessimistic, confident or insecure. Make it positive to show you are confident and capable. Consider this example:

I have to do systems analysis and planning for a lot of projects.

The tone is flat, "I have to" sounds negative and whiney, "do" is a dull verb, and "a lot of projects" is wishy-washy and inexact. The tone and impression given is "This applicant is not very professional and, furthermore, doesn't care." Read this rewrite:

As the primary manager for systems analysis and planning for four projects, I oversee six systems analysts.

How is the revised sentence an improvement? Don't you think the author:

▶ presents a more positive tone (direct, no whining)?
▶ sounds like a mover-and-shaker (*primary manager; I oversee six systems analysts*)?
▶ chooses powerful words suggesting leadership (*primary, manager, oversee*)?
▶ gives exact detail (*four projects, six systems analysts*)?

Here is a second pair of KSA sentences for you to analyze:

VERSION A: *I am the sole person to exercise full authority, unilaterally make major decisions, and keep commitments of a binding nature in all aspects and areas related to the vital NPF project.*
VERSION B: *I hold authority for major decisions and commitments in all areas of the NPF project.*

Check out the attitude in Version A! Isn't the tone pompous and overblown? In the rewrite, however, the tone has become upbeat and confident—but not conceited. And Version B avoids being unnecessarily complex, yet all the facts are there.

There is a fine line between sounding confident and sounding conceited. With practice (and the help from the people who read or listen to your drafts), you will find the right tone. To convey the most professional tone:

▶ Focus on the positive, rather than the negative.
▶ Give attention to what exists, not what is lacking.
▶ Convey a confident and in-charge attitude.

Double check that your tone does not sound:

▶ negative or critical of coworkers or superiors
▶ casual, uncaring, or frivolous
▶ pompous
▶ whiney or victimized

▶ KEEP IT BRIEF AND CLEAR: SEVEN GUIDELINES

The selecting officials reading your KSA information may have to read many other applications. They will be grateful to you if your writing is detailed and complete—and yet to the point. In other words, *do not use five words when two will get your message across.* Please review the following seven guidelines promoting brevity and clarity in your KSA writing.

Guideline #1: Be brief.

On writing clear and compelling KSA statements, do not waste your readers' time by taking too long to convey your message. There are a number of overused words and phrases that you should eliminate from your writing because they are awkward, unnecessary, or better altered to a shorter form.

Consider four of the worst offenders:

1. *Because of the fact that.* In most cases, just *because* will do.
   NO: *Because of the fact that the project ended prematurely, I moved on to my next assignment.*
   YES: *Because the project ended prematurely, I moved on to my next assignment.*

2. *That* and *which* clauses. Eliminate them by turning the idea in the *that* or *which* phrase into an adjective:
   NO: *This was a work experience that was very helpful.*
   YES: *This was a very helpful work experience.*

   NO: *My organizational meeting, which lasted five hours, ended at 4 o'clock.*
   YES: *My five-hour organizational meeting ended at 4 o'clock.*

3. *There is, this is,* and *it is.* These constructions avoid the direct approach and are often unnecessary. Instead, use a clear agent of action:
   NO: *It is with regret that I must close this branch.*
   YES: *I regret that I must close this branch.*

   NO: *There was no reason we co-workers could find to disagree.*
   YES: *We co-workers could find no reason to disagree.*

4. *That* by itself is a word often cluttering sentences, as in the following example:
   NO: *Mr. Hageman said that he thought that my workshop was useful and that he was happy that there will be a follow-up meeting.*
   YES: *Mr. Hageman said he thought my workshop was useful, and he was happy there will be a follow-up meeting.*

The following table presents words and phrases that are awkward or too wordy, as well as suggested substitutions. If you like, use a separate piece of paper to write out a sentence using phrases from the right column. Through practice, you will attain an eye for good, concise writing.

WORD CHOICES FOR CONCISE WRITING

Wordy	Replace with
a lot of	*many* or *much*
all of a sudden	*suddenly*
along the lines of	*like*
are able to	*can*
as a matter of fact	*in fact*, or Delete
as a person	Delete
as a whole	Delete
as the case may be	Delete
at the present time	*currently* or *now*
basic necessity	*necessity*
both of these	*both*
by and large	Delete
by definition	Delete
compare and contrast	*compare*
due to the fact that	*because*
final destination	*destination*
for all intents and purposes	Delete
has a tendency to	*often* or Delete
has the ability to	*can*
in order to	*to*
in the event that	*if*
in the near future	*soon*
is able to	*can*
it is clear that	Delete
last but not least	*finally*
on a daily basis	*daily*
on account of the fact that	*because*
particular	Delete
period of time	*period* or *time*
somewhere in the neighborhood of	*about*
take action	*act*
the fact that	*that*, or Delete
the majority of	*most*
the reason why	*the reason* or *why*
through the use of	*through*
totally obvious	*obvious*
with regard to	*about* or *regarding*
with the exception of	*except for*

Guideline #2: Be clear and specific.

Use specifics and details to substantiate your comments. Look at the following examples.

VAGUE: *Our investment in time and training increased productivity significantly in the following months.*

CLEAR/SPECIFIC: *The Procurement team's investment in time and training increased productivity by 80% during March–August, 2002.*

VAGUE: *Our new system's set-up was somewhat behind schedule.*

CLEAR/SPECIFIC: *Our new system's set-up was one week late.*

HELPFUL HINT—USE POWERFUL, PRECISE ADJECTIVES AND ADVERBS

Add these powerful phrases to add to your KSA and resume vocabulary file:

directly involved

unflagging dedication

promptly accepted

productive meeting

influential employee

invaluable asset

priceless decision

Guideline #3: Do not repeat yourself.

Another way to annoy or lose your reader is to be **redundant** by stating an idea or piece of information more than once. Writers repeat themselves unnecessarily because they are not sure that they have been clear, or they are not attentive to the need to be concise. Be concise the first time, and repetition will not be a problem. Consider these examples:

REDUNDANT: *As bookkeeper, I gave a detailed summary every day at 4:00 P.M. in the afternoon.*

CONCISE: *As bookkeeper, I gave a detailed summary every day at 4:00 P.M.*

Note that *P.M.* means "in the afternoon," so there is no reason to say *in the afternoon*. It's both a waste of words and the reader's time.

REDUNDANT: *My innovative flagging system was yellow in color to contrast with the files.*

CONCISE: *My innovative flagging system was yellow to contrast with the files.*

REDUNDANT: *It was time to terminate the project and put an end to it.*

CONCISE: *It was time to terminate the project.*

REDUNDANT: *I instructed my clients to please let me know their plans as soon as possible and at their earliest convenience.*

CONCISE: *I instructed my clients to please let me know their plans as soon as possible.*

Guideline #4: Eliminate Ambiguity.

Ambiguity means having two or more possible meanings. The problem with ambiguous language is that the meaning understood by the reader *may not be the one intended* by the writer. Try not to confuse your readers by using the wrong words or by using the right words in the wrong order. How to do this?

▶ Avoid using words with **ambiguous meanings**, meanings that are not immediately clear.

AMBIGUOUS: *As the MTA photographer, I shot the foreman.*

The sentence can have two meanings: You, the MTA photographer, shot photographs of the foreman using your camera, or you shot the foreman with a gun. If the meaning is the first one, here is one possible rewrite:

CLEAR: *As the MTA photographer, I took pictures of the foreman.*

Another example:

AMBIGUOUS: *One problem I saw in Precinct 12 was that our new police artist drew attention.* (*artist, drew*—get it?)

CLEAR: *One problem I saw in Precinct 12 was that our new police artist attracted attention.*

▶ Avoid **misplaced modifiers**, words or phrases that describe something, but are in the wrong place in the sentence.

AMBIGUOUS: *The woman moved the forklift with the hard hat.*

Here, the *word order* of the sentence, not an individual word, causes the confusion. Did the woman wear a hard hat? Did the forklift wear a hard hat? Did the woman move the forklift using her hard hat? Because the phrase *with the hard hat* is in the wrong place (a misplaced modifier), the meaning of the sentence is unclear. Try instead:

CLEAR: *The woman with the hard hat moved the forklift.*

In the previous example, we merely moved the modifier *with the hard hat* to the better place in the sentence. Here is another example:

AMBIGUOUS: *In 2000, after my industrial accident at Peck's Warehouse, I went to see the doctor with a severe headache.*

CLEAR: *In 2000, after my industrial accident at Peck's Warehouse, I went to see the doctor because I had a severe headache.*

(Note: In this case, you are *adding* words to craft a clearer sentence.)

▶ Avoid **dangling participles,** phrases with a verb ending in *–ing*, that do not refer to the subject of the sentence it modifies.

AMBIGUOUS: *While working on the annual financial report, my colleague's computer crashed.*

(Was the computer working on the report?)

CLEAR: *While my colleague was working on the annual financial report, his computer crashed.*

Note that correcting a dangler involves adding and/or rearranging the words in a sentence to make the meaning clear. Consider this example:

AMBIGUOUS: *While reading the morning agenda, the noisy elevator distracted my team leader.*

CLEAR: *While my team leader was reading the morning agenda, she was distracted by the noisy elevator.*

OR

The noisy elevator distracted my team leader while she was reading the morning agenda.

Guideline #5: Avoid unclear pronoun references.

Another common mistake that interferes with clarity is the use of unclear pronoun references. Pronouns should be used only when it is certain to whom they refer. (Pronouns, such as *me, you, he, she, his,* and *hers,* replace nouns. See Chapter 7 for more on parts of speech.) Study these examples:

UNCLEAR: *I went to the peer review with Ted and Fred, and we took his MC-4 badge.*

Whose badge? *His* could mean either Ted's or Fred's. The writer needs to use a proper name instead of the pronoun to eliminate the possibility the reader will not understand:

CLEAR: *I went to the peer review with Ted and Fred, and we took Ted's badge.*

UNCLEAR: *As a consequence of my action, Ms. Jones told Ms. James that she had found her missing report.*

CLEAR: *As a consequence of my action, Ms. Jones told Ms. James that she had found Ms. James' missing report.*

Now consider the sentence, *As an intern, I watched them sponsor a new tax law in January, 2003.* The pronoun error in this case involves using a vague *them*, when there are specific people behind an action, but the writer may or may not know exactly who those people are. If it is possible, be precise: *As an intern, I watched the state senators sponsor a new law in January, 2003.*

UNCLEAR: *They closed the conference center after they discovered several fire code violations.*

CLEAR: *The owners of the conference center closed their doors after the fire department discovered several fire code violations.*

Guideline #6: Beware of acronyms.

If you were a federal job reader, evaluating dozens of KSA statements, how would you react to the following:

As an EES for the DVA, I have been working closely for three months with my HROC in evaluating the Command's EEO Program. I gave advice on EEO federal guidelines and procedures, as well as suggested possible means of resolving the pre-complaint.

Isn't it difficult to understand? You probably noticed that the first sentence alone contains four acronyms. **Acronyms** are abbreviations, words formed by the first letter or letters of several words in a title. Sometimes an acronym itself spells a real word, such as **VISTA**, which stands for **V**olunteers **i**n **S**ervice **t**o **A**merica. Some acronyms do not form real words, but are pronounced as if they were real words, such as **FEMA** (FEE-muh), which stands for **F**ederal **E**mergency **M**anagement **A**gency.

In the excerpt above, the writer's current supervisor and coworkers will understand what *EES*, *DVA*, *HROC*, and *EEO* mean, but the KSA readers may not. Therefore, always spell out the first mention of an acronym, and then you may use acronym alone in subsequent references. Here is the revised excerpt:

As an Equal Employment Specialist (EES) for the Department of Veterans Affairs (DVA), I have been working closely for three months with my Human Resources Office Center (HROC) in evaluating the Command's Equal Employment Opportunity (EEO) Program. I gave advice on EEO federal guidelines and procedures, as well as suggested possible means of resolving the pre-complaint.

Guideline #7: Resist jargon: buzzwords, technobabble, legalese, and bureaucratese.

As with acronyms, jargon—such as buzzwords, technobabble, legalese, and bureaucratese—will probably bewilder your reader. Workplace **jargon,** or specialized language, should be avoided or used sparingly. (You will not get your message across efficiently if your reader has to consult a dictionary to understand what you have written!) These definitions and examples will help.

▶ Buzzwords

Buzzwords are real words, with real meanings, used in trendy ways. They can also be newly invented or euphemistic words ("He was down-sized" in place of "He was fired" springs to mind.) This type of business slang is at best pompous, and at worst, confusing. And, like other forms of slang, buzzwords do not belong in KSAs. Examples include: *resultful* (gets results), *suboptimal* (not the best), *guesstimate* (estimate), *leverage* (use), *modality* (method), and *right-sizing* (cutting excess).

▶ Technobabble

If you work in a field that constantly generates new words, or uses highly technical or field-specific language, you and your colleagues will undoubtedly use *technobabble* or *techno-jargon* in conversation and in writing for an audience of your peers. However, your jargon may confuse a KSA reader, especially if you are describing experiences in fields other than the field of the job you are applying for. Therefore, if you need to use jargon, explain yourself in words that will be understood by all.

Here is an example of technobabble:

I worked from 1998–2002 for GlobalCommand, a company that provides secure global communications through the following services: worldwide satellite connectivity; terrestrial-based, fault-tolerant networks; bandwidth-rich services at lower costs; Internet broadband access to remote locations; Voice-over IP (VoIP); redundancy prevention; Virtual Private Networks (VPNs); and streaming video and video conferencing.

Did you identify several words and phrases as techno-jargon? Maybe you understood a few terms more than others. Some technobabble candidates are *connectivity, terrestrial-based networks, fault-tolerant, bandwidth-rich services,* and so on. Such terms need to be translated for a non-technical audience *unless they directly relate to the KSA qualifications and the job sought.* In that case, you can assume your reader will be familiar with the technical jargon of that field.

▶ Legalese

Lawyers must also take care to avoid sounding pompous and confusing their audience. When writing to those who did not attend law school, avoid *legalese,* legal terms that are not commonly understood. Compare the first sentence with the second:

LEGALESE: *I transcribed court statements that said a duty of care to the herein above mentioned plaintiff was breached by the defendant when the slippery floor was left un-mopped by the defendant.*

CLEAR: *I transcribed court statements that said the defendant breached her duty of care to the plaintiff when she failed to mop the slippery floor.*

▶ **Bureaucratese**

Bureaucratese is a style of language characterized by government jargon and euphemisms, used by some bureaucrats. There is often an overuse of the passive voice, and the language sounds phony and confusing. Enjoy this exaggerated example of bureaucratese:

BUREAUCRATESE: *In September of that year, I determined the nature of how the OCP impacted the Board in a less-than-positive manner. I made an analyzation via the conduit of surveys and the required report. My recommendations and suggestions were subsequently prioritized and interfaced with measurable success.*

CLEAR: *In September 2004, I measured the negative impact of the Office of Civilian Personnel (OCP) on the Westland County Planning Board, through surveys I authored and administered to 38 employees. In November, I submitted a 15-page report with recommendations. These suggestions were implemented the following year, resulting in higher morale and 60% increased productivity.*

▶ **SUMMARY**

Showcase your knowledge, skills, and abilities in excellent KSA statements that are brief and clear. Resist slang and clichés, use appropriate formality, choose the active voice and a proactive vocabulary, consider denotation and connotation, convey a positive tone, and avoid ambiguities and jargon. Do not use too many words when a few will do, and do not waste time by repeating yourself. Your readers will appreciate the time and effort you spent on polishing your KSA writing.

7

Grammar, Spelling, Mechanics, and Usage

In addition to choosing the right words, writing well means following the rules of grammar and spelling. Although you will probably type your KSA response on a computer with grammar and spell checking programs, these high-tech helpers are not fool-proof. You still need to know the basic mechanics in order to write well.

Many people think that grammar and spelling are no longer relevant. This is, after all, the age of e-mail, instant messaging, rap, slang, and emoticons. Shortcuts seem to be more in vogue, for instance, than the proper use of the word *myself*. Good grammar seems stuffy. Not so! Good grammar, spelling, mechanics, and usage have remained important in both federal and private work worlds. It is one way that people, agencies, and even countries can communicate on an even playing field.

In Chapter 6 you saw how word choice, tone, denotation, connotation, and clarity affect your message. Here you will discover a few dozen rules and examples that apply to the majority of common grammar, usage, spelling, and mechanics errors in these areas:

- ▶ parts of speech
- ▶ noun/verb agreement
- ▶ sentence fragments and run-on sentences
- ▶ double negatives
- ▶ commonly confused and misused words
- ▶ spelling

▶ punctuation
▶ capitalization

▶ PARTS OF SPEECH

Do you know your adverbs from your adjectives? Recognizing the parts of a sentence helps you understand how you might build stronger, clearer sentences. The following table offers definitions and examples of those building blocks of language, the parts of speech.

Part of Speech	Function	Examples
noun	names a person, place, thing, or concept	*Emily, teacher, dog, happiness, Africa, vase, New York Avenue, weather* *Laverne took her resume to the interview.*
pronoun	takes the place of a noun so that noun does not have to be repeated (there are many kinds of pronouns: personal, demonstrative, indefinite, interrogative, reflexive, relative)	*I, you, he, she, us, it, they, this, that, mine, yours, his, hers, itself, themselves, somebody, anyone, what, who, which* *I, Connor Brown, completed their survey myself.*
verb	describes an action, occurrence, or state of being	*jump, becomes, is, seemed, clamoring, to relax* *The report appeared incomplete when I first saw it.*
helping verb	combines with other verbs (main verbs) to create verb phrases that help indicate tenses	*forms of be, do, and have; can, could, may, might, must, shall, should, will, would* *Sheila had been coming to meetings early.*
adjective	describes nouns and pronouns; can also identify or quantify	*orange, gloomy, tired, large, light, happy; that (e.g., that car); three; several (e.g., several dogs)* *Yesterday I carefully moved four very large, unopened boxes.*
adverb	describes verbs, adjectives, other adverbs, or entire clauses	*smoother, slowly, more quickly, least skillfully, always, not, never, quite, very, today, lately, late, soon* *Yesterday I carefully moved four very large, unopened boxes.*

preposition	expresses the relationship in time or space between words in a sentence	*of, in, on, by, to, at, with, under, against, except, across, around, above, between, below, beneath, underneath, beside, upon, during, before, after, toward, through, throughout, next to* *Between* March 3 and April 2, I drove *throughout* Kansas working *for* the Department *of* Defense.
conjunction	connects parts of a sentence; joins them together	Coordinating Conjunctions: *and, but, or, for, nor, yet, so* Subordinating Conjunctions: *after, although, as, as if, as long as, as though, because, before, even if, even though, if, if only, in order that, now that, once, rather than, since, so that, than, that, though, till, unless, until, when, whenever, where, whereas, wherever, while* Correlative Conjunctions (always in pairs): *not only . . . but also, both . . . and, neither . . . nor, either . . . or, not . . . but, whether . . . or, as . . . as* *As long as* I can remember, I have wanted to help people *and* animals, *but* not as a sociologist.
interjection	Word or phrase used to exclaim or protest or command (not used in formal writing)	*Wow!, oh, what the heck, OK!*

▶ NOUN/VERB AGREEMENT

Verbs should agree with their subjects. This means that a singular subject requires a singular verb; a plural subject requires a plural verb. The key here is to identify the subject of the sentence, determine whether it is singular or plural, and then choose a correct verb. Sometimes it is easier than others to identify the true subject of a verb. Study these examples:

John and Ned were my colleagues. [subject = *John, Ned*; therefore, a plural subject takes a plural verb]

One of the manager's children is visiting today. [subject = *one*, not *children*. *Children* is part of the prepositional phrase *of the children*, and **subjects are never found in prepositional phrases.** So, the subject is singular, and the verb must be singular (*is*, not *are*) to agree with *one*.]

When sentences become more complex, you will need to look more closely to determine how to make the subject and verb agree. Here are some basic guidelines that may help you:

▶ Verbs in the present tense for third-person, singular subjects (*he, she, it* and anything those words can stand for) have *s* endings. Other verbs do not add *s* endings. EXAMPLE: Sam keeps the books for the department.

▶ Sometimes modifiers will get between a subject and its verb, but these modifiers must not confuse the agreement between the subject and its verb. EXAMPLE: The supervisor, who has been convicted along with his five brothers on four counts of extortion, is finally going to prison.

▶ If a compound, singular subject is connected by *and*, the verb must be plural. EXAMPLE: Both the 10-speed and the hybrid are appropriate for the Homeland Security Department bike race.

▶ When a compound, singular subject is connected by *or* or *nor*, the verb must be singular. EXAMPLE: Neither the 10-speed nor the hybrid is appropriate for a trail race, however.

▶ If one plural and one singular subject are connected by *or* or *nor*, the verb agrees with the closest subject. EXAMPLE: Neither sore muscles nor a rainy day is going to stop me from taking part in the Homeland Security Department's race.

When the subject comes after the verb, subject-verb agreement can be tricky. In sentences that begin with *there is* and *there are*, for example, the subject comes after the verb. The verb (*is/are*) must agree with that subject. For example:

INCORRECT: *There are a good reason to file those papers.*
CORRECT: *There is a good reason to file those papers.*

INCORRECT: *Here's the statistics to prove it.*
CORRECT: *Here are the statistics to prove it.*

Be careful when choosing a verb to accompany indefinite pronouns:

▶ The indefinite pronouns *anyone, everyone, someone, no one, nobody* are always singular and, therefore, require singular verbs. EXAMPLE: Everyone has done his or her best to help the team.

▶ *Each* is often followed by a prepositional phrase ending in a plural word (*each of the workshops*), thus confusing the verb choice. *Each*, however, is always singular and requires a singular verb. EXAMPLE: Each of the workshops was worthwhile.

▶ Some indefinite pronouns, such as *all, none,* and *some,* are singular or plural depending on what they are referring to. EXAMPLES: All of the supplies are missing. Some of the water in the reservoir is gone.

▶ The pronouns *neither* and *either* are singular and require singular verbs, even though they seem to be referring to two things. EXAMPLES: Neither of the two traffic lights is working. Which drill do you want? Either is fine.

▶ Fractional expressions such as *half of, a part of, a percentage of, a majority of* are sometimes singular and sometimes plural, depending on the meaning. EXAMPLES: Two-thirds of the water samples were polluted. Two-thirds of the sand was covered in oil spill. Forty percent of the soldiers are on this base. Forty percent of the base is in quarantine.

There are a few other noun/verb agreement rules, but the ones you have just reviewed are the most relevant to KSA response writing.

HELPFUL HINT—USE FLASH CARDS

You might feel silly using flash cards, but they are convenient-to-use reminders of rules and exceptions. All you need is a pack of index cards and a pen.

- On the front of each card, write a word you want to learn or a rule you need to remember.
- For words, write the correct spelling on one side and the definition on the other. Either read the definition first, and then guess the word, spelling it correctly, or read the word first and then give the definition:

  side one: extrapolate
  side two: to estimate something unknown on the basis of known information

- For grammar rules, state the rule on one side of the index card. Give examples of the rule on the other, in the WRONG/RIGHT format when possible, notating or underlining relevant parts of the example.

  side one: subject and verb should agree in number
  side two:
    INCORRECT: The cooks and the head chef distributes the meals.
    CORRECT: The <u>cooks</u> <u>and</u> the <u>head chef</u> [they, pl.] distribute the meals.
    INCORRECT: One of my colleagues compile the data.
    CORRECT: <u>One</u> [sing.] of my colleagues compiles the data.

▶ SENTENCE FRAGMENTS AND RUN-ON SENTENCES

Two types of writing errors to be aware of are sentence fragments and run-ons.

Fragments

A **sentence fragment** is a group of words that, although it may be punctuated as a sentence, does not express a complete thought. A fragment may be a dependent clause passed off as a sentence. Fragments also can be phrases or parts of other sentences. Here are some sentences fragments:

At the office.
Worried a lot.
Can't go to the conference.
When we finished the paperwork.

Fragments are corrected by verifying that there is a subject, a verb, and a complete thought:

The law partners met at the office.
I worried a lot, but it was wasted energy.
Teresa can't go to the conference.
When we finished the paperwork, Dr. Feinman began her talk.

While fragments are not usually acceptable in general business writing, they are acceptable in resumes and in KSA responses, particularly in bulleted lists. What follows is an example of fragments used correctly in a resume. Also, see Chapter 9 for KSA response samples, some demonstrating acceptable fragment use.

OFFICE MANAGER, 1998–2002
Litton Enterprises, Inc.
Sherwood, IN
Supervised three employees; coordinated sales schedules; distributed marketing materials; scheduled media events; maintained inventory

Run-Ons

A **run-on sentence** is a group of independent clauses that are run together into one sentence without proper punctuation. There are usually several methods for repairing a run-on. Review these two examples of run-on sentences and their repairs:

INCORRECT: *My challenge was obvious I had to negotiate for a better bid.*
CORRECT: *My challenge was obvious. I had to negotiate for a better bid.* [break the run-on into two sentences] OR
CORRECT: *My challenge was obvious: I had to negotiate for a better bid.* [add a colon] OR
CORRECT: *My challenge was obvious, and I had to negotiate for a better bid.* [add a comma and a coordinating conjunction] OR
CORRECT: *Considering my challenge was obvious, I had to negotiate for a better bid.* [turn the first independent clause into a dependent clause]

INCORRECT: *We were hungry and my secretary was tired but we had to get to the staging area as soon as possible.*
CORRECT: *We were hungry and my secretary was tired, but we had to get to the staging area as soon as possible.* [add a comma and a coordinating conjunction] OR
CORRECT: *We were hungry and my secretary was tired. Nevertheless, we had to get to the staging area as soon as possible.* [divide into two sentences and add a transition] OR
CORRECT: *We were hungry and my secretary was tired; however, we had to get to the staging area as soon as possible.* [add a semicolon and the conjunctive adverb however]

▶ DOUBLE NEGATIVES

There is never a reason to use a double negative (for example, *Neither the nurse nor the patient advocate never used those procedures.*) Maybe you think that one negative is not enough to emphasize your point. So, you add another. Instead of adding emphasis to your point, however, you have made it less clear. Examine these sentences with double negatives and how they were amended.

INCORRECT: *My foreman didn't never post the regulations.*
CORRECT: *My foreman never posted the regulations.* OR
CORRECT: *My foreman didn't ever post the regulations.*

INCORRECT: *His assistant never wore nothing but black to work.*
CORRECT: *His assistant always wore black to work.* OR
CORRECT: *His assistant only wore black to work.* OR
CORRECT: *His assistant never wore any color but black to work.*

INCORRECT: *The study won't tell me nothing about our EPA practices.*
CORRECT: *The study won't tell me anything about our EPA practices.* OR
CORRECT: *The study tells me nothing about our EPA practices.*

BARELY OBVIOUS

There are more negatives than the obvious *no, not, never, neither,* and *nor.* Remember that *hardly* and *barely* are negatives, too. If you are using those words, you already have a negative, so do not double up.

INCORRECT: *My boss was on temporary disability because she couldn't barely walk after her accident.*
CORRECT: *My boss was on temporary disability because she could barely walk after her accident.* OR
CORRECT: My boss was on temporary disability because she couldn't walk after her accident.

▶ COMMONLY CONFUSED OR MISUSED WORDS

English is a very complex language, with the largest vocabulary of any language in the world. Naturally, it follows that words that look alike (*affect, effect*) or sound alike (*to, two, too*) can be confused or misused. Pay attention to the meaning of every word that you use in your writing. If you are unsure that the word you are using is correct, look it up in your dictionary.

Commonly Confused Words

When you misuse words, your writing suffers. One wrong word—using *illicit* when you mean *elicit*, for example—can completely change the meaning of an otherwise well-written KSA response. It can also result in making your reader question your intelligence. The following list presents alphabetized words and phrases that are frequently confused with similar words. To help you understand how to use these words, the list provides a definition of each word and an example of its usage.

a lot (n.) many (Note that *a lot* is two words.)
She owns a lot of computer programs.
allot (v.) to give or share in arbitrary amounts; to apportion
They will allot each speaker only five minutes.

accept (v.) to agree to; to receive
Carlos will accept your recommendation.
except (prep.) with the exclusion of; other than
All staff members attended except Marco and Nita.

addition (n.) increase; enlargement; part or thing added
The new addition to the hospital provides more office space for the medical staff.
edition (n.) an issue of a book or newspaper
The author is working on the second edition of his computer manual.

advice (n.) counsel
The college counselor's advice helped me.
advise (v.) to give advice; to inform
The attorney will advise you on the agency's rules.

affect (v.) to influence
Larry's new contract will affect his annual income.
effect (n.) the result or outcome (v.) to bring about
(n.) *All the employees felt the effect of the redistribution.*
(v.) *The new leadership will effect massive changes.*

all ready (adj.) completely prepared
The auditors are all ready to discuss their findings.
already (adv.) by or before a specified or implied time
Ms. Groening already called the bank officer.

all together (adj.) in a group; in unison

Will the various departments work all together so our goals are met?

altogether (adv.) completely or thoroughly

Raising the budget is altogether unwise in today's economy.

allude (v.) to refer to something not specifically mentioned

Did the article allude to her lack of interest in the new product without actually stating it?

elude (v.) to escape notice or detection

By changing the subject, he was able to elude criticism.

ascent (n.) the act of climbing or rising

The ascent to the top of the organization was difficult.

assent (v.) to agree or to accept a proposal or an opinion

I assent to your idea.

capital (n.) money invested

How much capital was invested in the business?

capitol (n.) a government building

She took her class to the capitol in Harrisburg.

choose (v.) to select based on judgment

They will choose Ted because of his skill and knowledge.

chose (v.) past tense of choose

Art chose Gloria to be on his assembly line.

cite (v.) to acknowledge; to quote as a reference

You were asked to cite directly from your resource book.

sight (n.) the ability to see; vision

Joe's sight has improved with the treatment.

site (n.) a place; a plot of land

On what site are you planning to build the archives?

complement (n.) anything that completes a whole; (v.) to complete or make perfect

(n.) *A complement of certified public accountants would enhance your staff.*

(v.) *Michelle's new program will complement the other programs.*

compliment (n.) recognition; praise; flattery; (v.) to praise

(n.) *The supervisor's compliment pleased the clerks.*

(v.) *Frank will compliment his employees when they work overtime.*

consul (n.) an official appointed by the government to live in a foreign city to attend to the interests of the official's country

The consul from France helped the French tourists who had lost their passports.

council (n.) group of people called together to provide counsel

The vote of the city council was divided.

counsel (n.) advice; (v.) to provide advice

(n.) *We must obtain legal counsel before we make a decision.*

(v.) *Who is going to counsel Beth on the matter?*

continual (adj.) taking place in close succession; frequently repeated

The continual interruptions annoyed the listeners.

continuous (adj.) without break or let up

The watercooler's continuous flow of drips annoyed the factory workers.

cooperation (n.) assistance; help

The cooperation of both parties is necessary in this situation.

corporation (n.) type of business organization

The four doctors formed a corporation to practice medicine.

decent (adj.) correct; proper

We will accept any decent bid for the tunnel excavation.

descent (n.) going from a high level to a lower level

The descent of the asset's value is quite remarkable.

dissent (n.) disagreement

The situation caused dissent between the client and the provider.

desert (v.) to abandon; (n.) a barren geographical area

(v.) *Do not desert a group of employees who needs your support.*

(n.) *Rob drove through the desert to get to the meeting.*

dessert (n.) a course at the end of a meal

The cooks at West Point served chocolate ice cream for dessert.

disburse (v.) to make payments; to allot

We will disburse the money after the project is completed.

disperse (v.) to distribute

Did they disperse the pamphlets at the conference?

assure (v.) to make sure

We assure you that you can count on our support.

ensure (v.) to make sure; to guarantee

Bail is set to ensure the appearance of defendants in court.

insure (v.) to secure from harm; to guarantee life or property
The company will not insure people who are poor risks.

envelop (v.) to surround; to cover completely
The fog will envelop the staging area at daybreak.
envelope (n.) containers for letters, reports, and so forth
Send the memorandum in an interoffice envelope.

farther (adj.) more distant
Her home is farther from the air force base than Art's home.
further (adv.) to a greater degree or extent
No further suggestions will be accepted.

forth (adv.) forward; onward
From that day forth, I arrived at the airport one hour before departure time.
fourth (adj.) any one of four equal parts; the item following the first three in a series
Randi is the fourth person to ask the same question.

hear (v.) perceive by the ear
Speak loudly so that everyone can hear you.
here (adv.) in or at this place
Are all the speakers here?

hoard (v.) to collect and keep
The clerk wanted to hoard all office supplies.
horde (n.) a huge crowd
A horde of people blocked the street to prevent entrance.

its (pron.) possessive pronoun form of it
When did you see its paw prints at the crime scene?
it's contraction for it is
It's supposed to rain the day of our federal job fair.

lay (v.) to place; to put (transitive verb—requires an object)
Lay the dictionary on my desk.
lie (v.) to recline; to remain (intransitive verb—no object required)
Glenn will lie down on the gurney the nurse prepared for him.

loose (adj.) not restrained; not fastened
  The police dogs are loose again despite all our efforts at training camp.
lose (v.) to fail to win; to be deprived of
  My colleagues and I play the lottery, but we always lose.

medal (n.) a badge of honor
  Faye deserves a medal for her assistance to others.
meddle (v.) to interfere
  Do not meddle in your supervisor's business.
metal (n.) a mineral substance
  That item is made from metal not wood.

passed (v.) past tense of pass
  Sashi passed the firefighter's examination with a high grade.
past (adj.) finished; gone by
  The past season was good for the local retailers.

personal (adj.) private; not public or general
  I try to be constructive without getting too personal in my comments.
personnel (n.) the staff of an organization
  A change in personnel is due the first of next month.

principal (n.) the amount of the money borrowed in a loan; the head official in a court proceeding or school; (adj.) most important or influential
  (n.) *The principal of the mortgage is about to be paid off. Ms. Landis is the new principal at the high school.*
  (adj.) *What is the principal procedure manual used on this project?*
principle (n.) a basic belief or truth
  Follow this principle to solve your first problem.

quiet (adj.) still; calm
  A librarian prefers quiet rooms to accommodate the readers.
quit (v.) to stop; to discontinue
  John will quit his job when he applies to graduate school.
quite (adv.) very or fairly; positively
  Miranda is quite ill and will not be able to attend the evaluation.

stationary (adj.) fixed; unmovable
  That huge piece of equipment is stationary.
stationery (n.) paper for letters and envelopes
  The agency is having new stationery printed.

taught (v.) past tense of teach

My client taught me how to be patient on the job.

taut (adj.) tight

Make sure that the ropes are taut in order to hold the items.

than (conj.) in comparison with; (prep.) except; besides

(conj.) *Sean is older than Maria.*

(prep.) *It was none other than Noi who wallpapered the office.*

then (adv.) at that time

We will be ready then to discuss another investment.

their (pron.) plural possessive form of they

Their reports are on the receptionist's desk.

there (adv.) in or at that place

Brainerd hesitates to go to there to have his jeep repaired.

they're contraction for they are

They're interested in traveling to Spain on business.

to (prep.) in the direction of

Go to the corner of South and Prescott Avenues.

too (adv.) also; excessively

Too many opinions are being offered.

two (adj.) the number 2

Two women are being added to the engineering team.

whether (conj.) if it be the case; in either case

Whether Toni comes by air or car, she will arrive on time.

weather (n.) atmospheric condition at a certain time and place

Currently, the weather is very nice; however, tomorrow it is supposed to rain.

your (pron.) possessive form of *you* (may be singular or plural)

(singular) *Your job evaluation arrived in the mail.*

(plural) *Let me help you people with your assignments.*

you're contraction for you are

You're very well qualified for the job!

Commonly Misused Words

Choosing the right words also means being aware of the many commonly misused ones. You may find examples of misused words in the media, on billboards and other signs, in speech, and in writing every day. In fact, even when used incorrectly, these words often sound acceptable to many writers. Take the time to learn their denotative meanings, and avoid an embarrassing goof-up in your resume and KSA responses.

Word	When to Use It
amount	used when you cannot count the items to which you are referring, and when referring to singular nouns
number	used when you can count the items to which you are referring, and when referring to plural nouns
anxious	nervous
eager	enthusiastic, or looking forward to something
among	used when comparing or referring to three or more people or things
between	used for two people or things
bring	moving something toward the speaker
take	moving something away from the speaker
can	used to state ability
may	used to state permission
each other	when referring to two people or things
one another	when referring to three or more people or things
e.g.	an abbreviation for the Latin "exempli gratia," meaning *free example* or *for example*
i.e.	an abbreviation for the Latin "*id est*," meaning *it is* or *that is*
feel bad	used when talking about emotional feelings
feel badly	used when talking about physically feeling something
fewer	when you can count the items
less	when you cannot count the items
good	an adjective, which describes a person, place, or thing
well	an adverb, which describes an action or verb
more	used to compare one thing to another
most	used to compare one thing to more than one other thing
that	a pronoun that introduces a restrictive (or essential) clause
which	a pronoun that introduces a non-restrictive (or unessential) clause

▶ SPELLING

Do you know your spelling weaknesses? Think about it for a few seconds. Do you have a tough time with double consonants? Do you confuse *–ance* and *–ence* endings? Are plurals your weakness? If spelling is a challenge for you, this section showcases multiple resources, books and websites, where you can learn the rules and exceptions and where you can practice what you learn.

Why is spelling correctly important on your KSA response, or in any business communication for that matter? Correct spelling shows you care about detail and precision, that you want to present the best "you" you can. Software spell checkers are very helpful, but they can misread a word and OK it (letting you use *their* when you meant *there*, for example). Furthermore, it is easy to make a spelling error in English: English is a very challenging language to spell in. Here are three reasons why:

1. English not often phonetic, as some other languages are.
   EXAMPLE: The letter combination *ough* is pronounced differently in each of these words: *bough, through, although, rough, ought, cough.*

2. There are many exceptions to the rules.
   EXAMPLE: The spelling rhyme "*i* before *e*, except after *c*, or when pronounced *ay*, as in *neighbor* and *weigh*." Even this rule's exceptions has exceptions! The combination "ei" has other pronunciations, such as in *height, heifer,* and *forfeit*. The rule also fails to apply to names: Sheila, Keith, etc.

3. A large percentage of English vocabulary is words or word roots borrowed from other languages with other spelling conventions.
   EXAMPLES: *alchemy* (Greek); *in lieu of* (French); *curriculum/curricula* (Latin); *kindergarten* (German); *algebra* (Arabic)

Troublesome Words

The following list represents 150 words that are often misspelled. Each word is presented spelled correctly. As you read through this list, you may find yourself surprised at some spellings. There are people out there who have been writing *calandar, jewelery,* or *millenium* for years!

You can guard yourself against misspelling these troublesome words by becoming familiar with their correct spelling. First, read through the list and make a note of any words that have surprising spellings. Then recite or write each of the words that you think you regularly misspell.

absence	cemetery
abundance	coincidence
accidentally	collectible (also *collectable*)
accommodate	committee
acknowledgment	comparative
acquaintance	completely
aggravate	condemn
alibi	congratulations
alleged	conscientious
ambiguous	consistent
analysis	convenient
annual	correspondence
argument	deceive
awkward	definitely
basically	dependent
boundary	depot
bulletin	descend
calendar	desperate
canceled (sometimes spelled cancelled)	development
cannot	dilemma

discrepancy	maintenance
eighth	maneuver
eighteenth	mathematics
eligible	millennium
embarrass	minuscule
equivalent	miscellaneous
existence	misspell
exuberance	negotiable
feasible	ninth
February	occasionally
fifth	occurred
forcibly	omission
forfeit	opportunity
formerly	outrageous
fourth	pamphlet
fulfill	parallel
grateful	perceive
grievance	permanent
guarantee	perseverance
guidance	personnel
harass	possess
hindrance	potato
ideally	precede
implement	preferred
independence	prejudice
indispensable	prevalent
inoculate	privilege
insufficient	procedure
interference	proceed
interrupt	prominent
jealousy	pronunciation
jewelry	quandary
judgment	questionnaire
leisure	receipt
length	receive
lenient	recommend
liaison	reference
lieutenant	referred
lightning	regardless
loophole	relevant
losing	religious

remembrance	supersede
reservoir	temperament
responsible	temperature
restaurant	truly
rhythm	twelfth
ridiculous	ubiquitous
roommate	unanimous
scary	usually
scissors	usurp
secretary	vacuum
separate	vengeance
souvenir	visible
specifically	Wednesday
sufficient	wherever

Visit Helpful Spelling and Vocabulary Websites

The following websites contain information that will help you to improve your writing. You will notice that several of these sites were designed for ESL (English as a Second Language) programs. These programs often offer clear, easy-to-understand explanations of the complexities of English grammar. Some sites to visit are:

www.dictionary.com—A useful online dictionary (plus, you can click through to a handy thesaurus).

www.m-w.com—Merriam Webster Online. This site has a number of interesting features that will make you forget you are trying to improve your spelling.

www.randomhouse.com/words/—Words @ Random. Here you will find crossword puzzles, quizzes, and dictionaries.

www.say-it-in-english.com/SpellHome.html—Absolutely Ridiculous English Spelling.

www.spelling.hemscott.net/—Useful advice on how to improve your spelling.

www.spellingbcc.com/indshtml—The Scripps Howard National Spelling Bee site contains "Carolyn's Corner" with weekly tips and information on spelling.

www.spellweb.com—This site will help you to pick the correct spelling of two versions of a word or phrase.

Business Terms

Learning the proper usage and spelling of business terms and buzzwords can benefit you in your KSA writing and in your career. Business books are excellent resources for learning to spell and understand business terms because they often include glossaries to augment their content. Business magazines and websites usually feature timely topics and will make use of current terms.

There are thousands of business sites on the Internet. Here is a short list to get you started:

Barron's Online: www.barrons.com

Bloomberg.com: www.bloomberg.com

Business Journals: www.bizjournals.com (you can personalize the site to your locality)

Business Week Online: www.businessweek.com

Career Journal from *The Wall Street Journal*: www.careerjournal.com

CNNfn Online: www.cnnfn.com

Fast Company Magazine Online: www.fastcompany.com

Hoover's Online: www.hoovers.com

Inc. Magazine Online: www.inc.com

Office.com: www.office.com

The Business Search Engine: www.business.com

The Wall Street Journal Online: www.wsj.com

The following list includes commonly used business terms. Look for their spelling pitfalls. Find the definitions of the unfamiliar terms in a dictionary or online.

Word	Pitfall
acquisition	*qui* in second syllable
arbitrage	Last syllable is *trage*, not *tage*
architecture	*-ure* ending
beneficiary	Don't forget the second *i*
capital	Not *capitol*
collusion	Double *l*
commercial	Double *m*
consortium	*-tium* ending
consumer	Ending is *-er*, not *-or*
deduction	Single *d* in second syllable
disclosure	*-ure* ending
discrimination	Single consonants throughout
entitlement	Don't forget the second *e*
equity	*-ity* not *-aty*
exempt	Don't forget the *p*
financial	Ending is *-ial*
fiscal	Single *s*, single *c*
forecast	Don't forget the *e*
franchise	Ending is *-ise* not *-ize*
harassment	Single *r*, double *s*
jargon	Ending is *-on* not *-en*
liability	Ending is *-ity* not *-aty*
nepotism	Second syllable is *po* not *pa*

organization	*z*, not *s*
perquisite	*per* not *pur* or *pre*
prospectus	Ending is -*us*
revenue	Second syllable is *ve*
subsidy	Second syllable is *si*
tenure	Single *n*, single *r*

Technical Terms

The technology sector has added many new words to the English language. To become more comfortable spelling these words, review the memory joggers in the vocabulary list that follows.

You can easily expand your knowledge of technology terms by visiting any of the several websites geared toward the high-tech world. Here are a few sites to consider:

CIO Magazine Online: www.cio.com

Government Technology: www.govtech.net

Information Technology Association of America: www.itaa.org

Internet.com—The IT Resource: www.internet.com

National Institute of Standards and Technology: www.nist.gov

Tech Web—The Business Technology Network: www.techweb.com

Technology & Learning: www.techlearning.com

Technology Review (MIT): www.techreview.com

Web Services Community Portal: www.webservices.org

The following list highlights commonly used technology terms. Study the spelling hints and find the definitions of the unfamiliar terms in a dictionary or online.

Word	Pitfall
applet	One *t*
application	Double *p*
bandwidth	One word
bitmap	One *t*
browser	One *s*
cache	Don't forget the *e*
cursor	Ending is -*or*, not -*er*
database	One word
development	No *e* after the *p*
domain	No final *e*
embedded	Not *imbedded*
encryption	Don't forget the *p*
frequency	Ending is -*ency*
function	Don't forget the *c*
hardware	One word

implementation	Starts with *im*, not *in*
interactive	No hyphen
interface	No hyphen
Internet	Always capitalized
intranet	Don't confuse it with *Internet*
keyword	One word
monitor	Ending is *-or*
multimedia	No hyphen
programming	Double *m*
research	Vowel combination is *ea*
rollover	One word
server	Ending is *-er*, not *-or*
software	One word
style sheet	Two words
validation	Ending is *-tion*
vector	Ending is *-or*, not *-er*

▶ PUNCTUATION

Punctuation marks—the period, question mark, exclamation point, comma, semicolon, colon, hyphen, dash, apostrophe, quotation marks, ellipses, parentheses, brackets, and slash—are standardized marks that clarify meaning for your reader. They serve as traffic signs, directing the reader to pause, connect, stop, consider, and go. Study the following marks to be sure you are using your traffic signs correctly.

REFERENCE MATERIALS

The punctuation rules in this section are abbreviated to apply to KSA-type writing. In truth, there are many additional grammar rules, guidelines, and exceptions. If you will be writing a lot as part of your new job, you should own a good writer's reference manual.

Learn more about grammar and usage in any of these excellent reference books: *The Chicago Manual of Style, 15th edition, The MLA Handbook,* or *The APA Publication Manual.*

Period

A **period (.)** is a mark that indicates a "full stop" at the end of a sentence or an abbreviation. When writing your KSA responses, you will probably use periods at these opportunities:

1. To show the end of a declaratory sentence: *The monitor was set for 120 pounds of pressure.*
2. At the end of a courteous request: *Please forward your response.*

3. To indicate abbreviations, decimals, and website addresses: *Dr. Smythe; 6:00 P.M.; etc.; 86.7 degrees; www.dhhs.gov*

Question Mark

You may not have need for a question mark in your KSA response. The **question mark (?)** gives notice that this is a direct question:

> *How many sections would be evaluated?*
> *Who will be manning the polling tables?*

Also, be careful *not* to put a question mark at the end of an indirect question:

> *The team leaders asked the line workers what they were doing.*
> *I asked my boss if he had a termination date in mind.*

Exclamation Point

The **exclamation point (!)** is placed at the end of an interjection or an exclamatory sentence to give emphasis: *Wow! You are some clever inventor!* You probably won't need this mark in KSA response writing, as it is an informal punctuation mark.

Comma

Commas (,) are used to create pauses, to clarify, and to separate different parts of sentences. In business writing, there are six basic rules for using commas:

1. to set off nonessential clauses
2. to set off sentence interrupters
3. to separate joined sentences
4. to set apart a series of words being presented as a group
5. to set off introductories
6. to separate elements of dates and addresses

Let's look at each rule individually:

1. Use a comma to set off nonessential clauses

A **nonessential clause** is one that can be removed from a sentence without changing the sentence's meaning. For example:

> My coworker Denise, *who is active in a local labor union,* is a fifth grade teacher.

If you remove the highlighted clause from the sentence, the basic meaning remains the same. This is because the clause is nonessential—it is additional information but not necessary to the basic sentence *My coworker Denise is a fifth grade teacher.*

2. Use a comma to set off sentence interrupters

A **sentence interrupter** is a kind of nonessential phrase. It can be removed from the sentence without changing the basic meaning. For example:

I, *however*, will attend a certification program in the fall.

Take out the highlighted interrupter and the basic meaning stays the same:

I will attend a certification program in the fall.

Some examples of sentence interrupters are:

additionally	in addition
as a rule	in any event
consequently	in conclusion
for example	in summary
for instance	moreover
hopefully	on the contrary
however	on the other hand
if possible	therefore

Another kind of sentence interrupter is the **appositive**, which renames what went before it (but is not a full clause, with its subject and verb). The appositives are italicized in the following examples:

That report, *the third one on the pile*, was requisitioned by the DOD.
My mentor in this process, *Sally St. Clair*, was present. OR
Sally St. Clair, *my mentor in this process*, was present.
The last seminar on my list, *How to Read Auto-Immune Symptoms*, was held in 2003.

Appositives are usually set off by commas. Two exceptions are when the appositive is a one-word name or the appositive is essential to the meaning of the sentence, which can be very subtle:

My coworker *Jane* sent the paperwork back. [no commas; one word appositive]
The proposal writer *Hiram Small* labored for three hours with the other proposal writers.
 [no commas; *Hiram Small* is essential in order to distinguish him from the others]

3. Use a comma to separate joined sentences

When you have two complete sentences connected with a conjunction such as *and, but, nor, so, for,* or *or*, put a comma in front of the *and, but, nor, so, for,* or *or*.

I filed forms for three years, *and* I began to set up a new filing system.

My instincts were to solve this problem quickly, *but* we only had two weeks before our deadline.

The ten other employees were late, so we proceeded without them.

4. Use a comma to set apart a series of words being presented as a group

This is known as a **serial comma**. It is used when you have a series of words; the last word is often preceded by *and* or *or*. Each word in a series should be separated by a comma. However, some workplaces do not use the final comma (the one before *and* or *or*. For example:

I traveled to the conference with *Ryan, Michelle, Brooke, and Lucille*. OR

I traveled to the conference with *Ryan, Michelle, Brooke and Lucille*

We sorted mail in *clean, well-ventilated, roomy* spaces.

5. Use a comma to set off introductories

An **introductory** can be a word, a phrase, or a clause. A comma is used to separate the introductory part from the main part of the sentence in order to clarify meaning. An introductory can also be a sentence interrupter that falls at the beginning of a sentence. Here are examples of introductory words, phrases, and clauses:

Exhausted, I walked up to the marketing easel.

Moreover, the results were astounding.

Hoping for the best, I negotiated with both partners.

Although it was a rainy day, I drove the van pool from one meeting to the next.

6. Use a comma to separate dates and addresses

Commas may be used to separate parts of dates or places:

I was born on *October 21, 1950*, in the industrial city of *Cleveland, Ohio*.

Please send the application to *Marty Hayes, 1226 Main Street, Anaconda, CA 90010*

Semicolon

Generally, **semicolons (;)** are used to separate independent clauses and to separate items in a series that contains commas. Consider these guidelines and examples.

1. Use semicolons to separate independent clauses

FIRST CASE: Use a semicolon to separate independent clauses joined without a conjunction.

EXAMPLE: Four people worked on the project; only one received credit for it.

SECOND CASE: Use a semicolon to separate independent clauses that contain commas, even if the clauses are joined by a conjunction.

EXAMPLE: The strays were malnourished, dirty, and ill; but Liz had a weakness for kittens, so she adopted them all.

THIRD CASE: Use a semicolon to separate independent clauses that are connected with a conjunctive adverb that expresses a relationship between clauses.

EXAMPLE: Victoria was insubordinate; therefore, she was fired.

HELPFUL HINT—CONJUNCTIVE ADVERBS

Conjunctive adverbs connect independent clauses. They require a semicolon before and a comma afterward. Here are the most common ones:

however

moreover

nevertheless

therefore

EXAMPLE: The committee members met late; *nevertheless*, they compiled most of the survey.

2. Use semicolons to separate items in a series that already contains commas

This use helps readers to understand which sets of items go together. For example:

The dates for our seminars are Monday, January 10; Tuesday, April 14; Monday, July 7; and Tuesday, October 11.

I have worked in Omaha, Nebraska; Nutley, New Jersey; Amherst, Massachusetts; and Pensacola, Florida.

Colon

Colons (:) are used to introduce and to show an equivalent relationship (almost like an equals sign in math). Follow these guidelines:

1. Use colons to introduce

FIRST CASE: Use a colon to introduce a list of items.

EXAMPLE: These were the options for certification: *Electronic Mechanic, Electronic Industrial Controls Mechanic*, and *Electronic Measurement Equipment Mechanic*.

SECOND CASE: Use a colon to introduce a formal quotation.

EXAMPLE: One of my favorite sayings is from Woody Allen: "70% of success in life is show-
ing up."

THIRD CASE: Use a colon to introduce a word, phrase, or clause that equates to the main
part of the sentence—sort of like an equals sign in math.

EXAMPLE: My 60-pound weight loss was the result of one thing: an excellent exercise regimen.

[Here, *one thing = an excellent exercise regimen.*]

2. Use colons to show relationship

FIRST CASE: Use a colon between two independent clauses when the second explains the
first.

EXAMPLE: My supervisor ignored the telephone: He was afraid it was this troublesome
ex-employee.

SECOND CASE: Use a colon between the title and subtitle of a book.

EXAMPLE: *Dental Care: A Basic Text for Dental Hygienists*

THIRD CASE: Use a colon between volumes and page numbers.

EXAMPLE: *Scientific American* IV: 453

FOURTH CASE: Use a colon between hours, minutes, and seconds.

EXAMPLES: 2:00 P.M.; 1:23:31

Hyphen

To indicate word division at the end of a sentence, **hyphens (-)** used to be handwritten or typed on a
typewriter. These days, computers with word processing software insert hyphens for word division (though
some have trouble with words like *resign* and *antidiscrimination*). Therefore, in your proofreading stage,
check the automatic hyphenations your computer has inserted.

Here are other uses for hyphens:

▶ creating compound words, particularly modifiers *before* nouns, such as *well-known* scientist
and *out-of-date* curriculum
▶ writing numbers *twenty-one* to *ninety-nine* and fractions, such as *five-eighths*, *one-fourth*
▶ adding certain prefixes to words:
  1. When a prefix comes before a capitalized word or the prefix is capitalized, use a hyphen:
     non-English, A-frame, I-formation
  2. The prefixes *self-*, *all-*, and *ex-* nearly always require a hyphen: *ex-husband, all-inclusive, self-
     control*

3. When a prefix ends with the same letter that begins the word, you will often use a hyphen (*anti-intellectual, de-emphasize*), but not always (*unnatural, coordinate, cooperate*).

4. Sometimes in a series of compound words, the hyphen acts as a sort of "placeholder" with a space or comma after it until the final term: *Both full- and part-time employees were hired; The 2-, 3-, and 4-year-old capsules had to be replaced.*

Note: There is no space between a hyphen and the character on either side of it.

Dash

Dashes (—) are "interruption marks" usually created by typing two hyphens in a row. They do not exist as a substitute for commas, colons, or semicolons. Rather, dashes are punctuation marks that should be used cautiously and only for a few specific situations in business. These three circumstances are:

1. to signify an interruption of thought or to insert a comment
2. to emphasize exposition
3. to connect a beginning phrase or list to the rest of a sentence

Study these examples of dash usage:

1. To signify an interruption of thought or to insert a comment

I remember exactly where I was and what I was doing—what American wouldn't?—when the World Trade Center was attacked.

2. To emphasize exposition

Keeping a list of your daily inventory outlay—copier paper, pads, pens, and files—is a helpful way to track what to reorder.

Good time-management skills—planning, prioritizing, and following-through—are essential for managers.

3. To connect a beginning phrase or list to the rest of a sentence

Pride of New York—that is the agriculture program in which I am interested.

Tenacity, diplomacy, and charm—those qualities are what you need to be a good fundraiser.

Note: There is no space between a dash and the character on either side of it.

Apostrophe

An **apostrophe (')** is generally used in four cases, as stated here. The first two occasions may well be part of your KSA response writing; the second two will probably not be.

Use an apostrophe:

1. to create possessives: dog's bone; Frank's; child's; children's; the witness' view
2. as part of a proper name: Donald O'Connor; Louis L'Amour; D'Artagnan

3. to indicate missing letter(s) in a contraction: I'm (I am); can't (cannot); she'd (she would); it's (it is; not the same word as the possessive pronoun *its*)

4. to form plurals in a very few cases, when the word could otherwise be misunderstood: Don't forget to dot your *i*'s; There are three *a*'s in *banana*. [but no apostrophes in these cases: six Smiths in the room; 1980s; CPAs]

Quotation Marks

Quotation marks (" ") set off material that is quoted or spoken. They always travel in pairs. For example:

> I received a citation saying, "Sgt. Malloy has a strong working knowledge of the complicated Ram-Air Parachute System."
> My line manager told me to be "extra, extra" careful.

Do not enclose *indirect quotations* in quotation marks:

> The CEO said that NAFTA will eventually benefit even small companies. (indirect quotation)
> The CEO said, "NAFTA will eventually benefit even small companies." (direct quotation)

Quotation marks are also used to indicate titles of chapters, sections of reports, poems, stories, articles, and songs:

> I authored the "Uses for Widgets" section of the report.

Other Punctuation Marks with Quotations

As for placement of punctuation marks within or without the quotation marks, in the United States, we always put a comma or a period *inside* the final quotation mark, regardless of the logic:

> Ms. Vandermeer told me my work was "extraordinary," and then we finished my review.
> He recommended the chapter called "Electrician's Safety."

However, with all other punctuation marks, logic is followed:

> Do you like the chapter entitled "Electrician's Safety"? (The question is the whole sentence, not within the title.)
> Ms. Dodsen yelled "Stop the printer!" (The exclamation is part of the quotation.)
> I put classical music on the intercom, such as "Claire de Lune"; subsequently, my colleagues became more productive. (The semicolon is not part of the song title.)

Ellipsis

You may never need to use it, but an **ellipsis** (. . .) proves to be a handy device if you are quoting material and are omitting some words. The ellipsis consists of three evenly spaced periods with spaces between the ellipsis and surrounding letters or other marks.

Take the sentence "Our ceremony honored twelve brilliant athletes from the Caribbean who were visiting the United States." and leave out "from the Caribbean who were":

The ceremony honored twelve brilliant athletes . . . visiting the United States.

If the omission comes after the end of a sentence, the ellipsis will be placed after the period, making a total of four dots.

Parentheses

A pair of **parentheses** (( )) surrounds words that you want to de-emphasize or that would not normally fit into the flow of your text, but you want to include nonetheless. Scan these examples:

As a secretary at Brooke Medical Center (2001–02), I performed various duties.
I earned the South African Defense Force (SADF) Rigger Badge.
I have experience writing a range of communications (memos, procedures, reports, and evaluations, for example).

Note that if the material within parentheses appears within a sentence, do not use a capital letter or period to punctuate that material, even if the material is itself a complete sentence:

We proceeded with the itinerary (we had already filled out the necessary paperwork).

Brackets

Brackets ([ ]) should be used sparingly. The two most common uses would be these:

1. Within a set of parentheses

I had finished the environmental study for Dr. Tom Middleswart (my first employer [1994]).

2. To make an editorial comment or change

The agency claimed it was *relying on CIA intelligence reports* to support its opinions of the security situation [italics mine].
Mrs. Espinoza charged her former employer with "falsification of [her] coaching record."

Slash

The **slash** or **slant** (/) is most often used to mean *or* (*I took a pass/fail test. Each architect took his/her blueprints home.*). Also, a slash can be part of a URL (website address): http://www.learnatest.com.

▶ CAPITALIZATION

Here are the six basic occasions that require capitalization:

- ▶ the first word of a sentence: *My supervisor walked in.*
- ▶ proper nouns (specific names of people, places, and things): *The Treasury Department representative, John Bellew, was in Stamford.*
- ▶ the first word of a complete quotation, but not a partial quotation: *She told me to "Use your best judgment."*
- ▶ the first, last, and other important words of a title: *The manual we wrote was* Internet Websites for Health Department Resources.
- ▶ languages, religions, ethnicities, nationalities, course titles: *My favorite teacher was a French national who taught a course called Islamic Literature 101.*
- ▶ The pronoun *I* and any contractions made with it: *I'm certain that I learned how to negotiate better from this experience.*

HELPFUL HINT—DO NOT CONFUSE PROPER NOUNS AND COMMON NOUNS

Proper nouns require capitalization. Common nouns do not. How can you tell the difference? A **proper noun** is specific, referring to a specific person (Juanita), place (England), or thing (Nissan). A **common noun** is general, referring to a general group of people (woman), place (country), or thing (vehicle).

▶ SUMMARY

Writing strong KSA responses means comprehending, then following the rules of grammar, usage, and mechanics. In this chapter you absorbed a few dozen rules that apply to these important subjects: parts of speech, noun/verb agreement, sentence fragments and run-on sentences, double negatives, commonly confused and misused words, spelling, punctuation, and capitalization.

First Draft to Final Draft of Your KSAs

At last it is time to sit down and flesh out the outline you sketched in Chapter 5. You are ready to go from first draft to final draft. Recall that the most potent KSA responses:

► use the Challenge-Context-Action-Result (CCAR) model
► include specific examples of experience
► focus on results

Your tasks to reach these goals are **formatting**, **writing**, and **revising and editing**.

You are now ready to choose how you want to format your paragraphs and pages—or, you may have already selected a format while outlining in Chapter 5, so that your outline reflected your format choice. If it helps, scan the many examples of KSA responses in Chapter 9. Do not look at their content for now, just their formatting. Considering the examples you have chosen for your KSA response, which of the following elements are in the "look" you like best?

> ► headings and subheadings?
> ► lots of white space or not so much?
> ► short or long paragraphs?
> ► bulleted lists?
> ► numbered lists? unnumbered lists?
> ► effective use of ALL-CAPS, *italics*, or **boldface**?

Why even care about paragraph and page formatting? Because paragraphs that are easy to absorb clarify your writing, while lessening the reader's eye strain. First, some general guidelines for writing a KSA response:

▶ Present CCAR elements—context, challenge, action, and results—in a different order if that suits your message.

▶ Understand that there may be more than one of each CCAR element, for example, two challenges within one context or several results from several actions.

▶ Keep your paragraphs brief—usually between five and ten lines—depending on their content.

▶ Type your text in a readable format.

Consider examples of the three most common formats for KSA responses: **short paragraphs**, **subheadings**, and **bulleted lists**. (The following examples might represent the content part of one CCAR-model response.)

Short Paragraph

As a dental assistant at Blair Dental Clinic in Alabama (2001–02), I served as first surgical assistant and scrub assistant to the surgeons in surgical procedures. I assisted in minor surgeries, maintaining and disinfecting all equipment and instruments, holding and handling instruments, performing retraction, and holding and cutting sutures.

Subheadings

While dental assistant at Blair Dental Clinic in Alabama (2001–02), I was responsible for:

Pre-Surgical Procedures. As first surgical assistant and scrub assistant, I maintained, and disinfected all equipment and instruments, using both cold and hot sterilization methods.

Minor Surgery Assist. I held and handled instruments, performing retraction, and holding and cutting sutures.

Bulleted List

While dental assistant at Blair Dental Clinic in Alabama (2001–02), I was responsible for:

■ **Pre-Surgical Procedures.** As first surgical assistant and scrub assistant, I maintained, and disinfected all equipment and instruments, using both cold and hot sterilization methods.

■ **Minor Surgery Assist.** I held and handled instruments, performing retraction, and holding and cutting sutures.

HELPFUL HINT—WHITE SPACE

KSAs are usually each one to one and a half pages, single spaced. For readability, be sure there is some white space. For example, make the page lengths a little less than a full page, so there is some white space at the bottom of the page. If you write about two examples, make each example two paragraphs, with a total of four paragraphs—there will be some white space between paragraphs.

As you will discover in Chapter 9, there are several formatting styles—and combinations of formats. At last, you have reached the point of no return—it is time to sit down and write the first draft of your KSA response.

▶ SITTING DOWN AND WRITING

Soon it will be time to put pen to paper—or keystroke to monitor screen. Either at this point or at the end of this section, return to Chapter 9 to read the *content* of some of the sample KSA requirements and responses. These sample job listings have been chosen from all six federal job categories and for various entry levels. Reading as many examples as you can helps you in choosing your own presentation and style.

How do you move from the notes and outline you made in Chapter 5 to a full-blown KSA response such as the examples in Chapter 9?

From Outline to Text

Please reread these reprinted notes from Chapter 5, which are followed by the KSA response that evolved from the notes. Following the response are six steps to take you from outline to text.

Sample Outline and Notes

KSA = *Ability to work and cooperate with others, interact tactfully, and be responsive to a culturally diverse workplace.*

I. [Example] Chester Brown and his negative attitude

    A. [Context] acting supervisor, Lake Ave St., Altadena; 2 months; veteran employee bitter, angry; disliked management; coworkers dislike him

    B. [Challenge or Goal] turn Chester around; bring out his positives; help coworkers appreciate him; encourage working together in diversity

    C. [Action] encouraged respect for him; join us for breakfast, asked him questions; involved in daily operations; Safety Captain thing; wrote complaint letter to telephone company for him

    D. [Results] Chester was happier; contributed to team; others began to respect him, invited to breakfast; became more open to him; I communicate/cooperate with others and motivate coworkers to do same; I am tactful, I could find his skills (safety, experience), accept diversity (cranky, older employee)

Sample KSA Response Based on Outline

Ability to work and cooperate with others, interact tactfully, and be responsive to a culturally diverse workplace.

While acting supervisor for two months at the Lake Avenue Postal Station in Altadena, CA, I encountered a veteran letter carrier who exhibited a very angry and dispirited attitude toward his job. [CONTEXT] The carrier had a general mistrust of management, from, according to the carrier, "years of autocratic and abusive mismanagement." Our coworkers avoided this person. [CHALLENGE] Through my daily actions, I was able to turn an apparent negative into a positive by involving this carrier in the station's day-to-day operations. If I did not know the answer to a question, I would ask this carrier since he had years of postal experience. I encouraged our coworkers to invite him to our breakfast break, where we learned he had some fascinating experiences. I activated his concern for safety by encouraging him to volunteer for Safety Captain, a job where he gave weekly safety talks to the other carriers. I believe the other workers saw that I valued the older carrier's experience, and they also learned from him. [ACTION] Through my actions and others, the results were an employee who contributed to the team concept and other team members who were not discouraged by a negative colleague. By tactfully working with this employee and our coworkers on a daily basis, I demonstrated that I was concerned with both postal operations and my fellow postal employees. Together, we grew to appreciate and work among a diversity of ages and attitudes. [RESULTS]

What are the writer's six steps in this process from outline to text?

1. **The writer selects the details from the outline** that are most consistent with the KSA requirement and most relevant to her story. For example, she deletes Chester's name and she decides not to use the note about helping Chester write a complaint letter to the telephone company.
2. **The writer writes out her response, using the CCAR model.** In this case, the response is structured in context-challenge-action-results model, but it does not have to be.
3. **The writer repeatedly refers back to the KSA requirement** to be sure she places some of the same or similar vocabulary into her response (*team, tactful, diversity*).
4. **The writer *adapts*** her abilities and experiences to meet broadly similar requirements. In this case, she does *not* have a culturally diverse situation at her postal station, but she does have age diversity (Chester is an older man with a lot of experience; the other workers are younger and less experienced) and attitude diversity (Chester is negative and bitter; the others are not). The writer indicates she is comfortable and can encourage others to be comfortable in a diverse team.
5. **The writer confirms that she addresses all of the KSA requirement** (in this case, three parts: ability to cooperate; tactful interaction; responsive to diversity).
6. **The writer adds something to her response to set herself apart from (and superior to) other applicants.** In this example, the writer explains that she has been a supervisor (acting)

for two months. She also demonstrates that she has not only the "ability to work and cooperate with others," but *has the skills to inspire coworkers to do the same.*

YOUR OWN MODEL CCAR

- If the flow of writing is more effective, write the challenge before the context, or choose any other configuration that feels natural to the particular response.
- Do not type the words *Context*, *Challenge*, or *Action* to indicate those sections of your KSA. You may, however, type the word *Results*, so the reader can find the results quickly. Everyone wants to read the results.

Leadership Language

If you are applying for a leadership position (executive, supervisor, trainer, foreman, manager, team leader, head planner, lead engineer, etc.), you may benefit by reviewing the five Leadership Competency Definitions as defined by the Office of Personnel Management (OPM). You can find this information at www.opm.gov/ses. Federal evaluators look for these qualities, listed here, in KSA responses to leadership job postings.

However, please recognize that *many of these competencies—such as integrity, flexibility, and interpersonal skills—are desirable in applicants* for any federal position. Read the Leadership Language section below to borrow some of the power words and proactive phrases from these definitions for your particular KSA response.

Leadership Language

1. **Leading Change**

   Continual Learning—Grasps the essence of new information; masters new technical and business knowledge; recognizes own strengths and weaknesses; pursues self-development; seeks feedback from others and opportunities to master new knowledge.

   Creativity and Innovation—Develops new insights into situations and applies innovative solutions to make organizational improvements; creates a work environment that encourages creative thinking and innovation; designs and implements cutting-edge programs/processes.

   External Awareness—Identifies and keeps up to date on key national and international policies and economic, political, and social trends that affect the organization. Understands near-term and long-range plans and a competitive business advantage in a global economy.

   Flexibility—Is open to change and new information; adapts behavior and work methods in response to new information, changing conditions, or unexpected obstacles. Adjusts rapidly to new situations warranting attention and resolution.

   Resilience—Deals effectively with pressure; maintains focus and intensity and remains optimistic and persistent, even under adversity. Recovers quickly from setbacks; effectively balances personal life and work.

Service Motivation—Creates and sustains an organizational culture which encourages others to provide the quality of service essential to high performance. Enables others to acquire the tools and support they need to perform well. Shows a commitment to public service. Influences others toward a spirit of service and meaningful contributions to mission accomplishment.

Strategic Thinking—Formulates effective strategies consistent with the business and competitive strategy of the organization in a global economy. Examines policy issues and strategic planning with a long-term perspective. Determines objectives and sets priorities; anticipates potential threats or opportunities.

Vision—Takes a long-term view and acts as a catalyst for organizational change; builds a shared vision with others. Influences others to translate vision into action.

2. Leading People

Conflict Management—Identifies and takes steps to prevent potential situations that could result in unpleasant confrontations. Manages and resolves conflicts in a positive, constructive manner to minimize negative impact.

Leveraging Diversity—Recruits, develops, and retains a diverse high-quality workforce in an equitable manner. Leads and manages an inclusive workplace that maximizes the talents of each person to achieve sound business results. Respects, understands, values and seeks out individual differences to achieve the vision and mission of the organization. Develops and uses measures and rewards to hold self and others accountable for achieving results that embody the principles of diversity.

Integrity/Honesty—Instills mutual trust and confidence; creates a culture that fosters high standards of ethics; behaves in a fair and ethical manner toward others, and demonstrates a sense of corporate responsibility and commitment to public service.

Team Building—Motivates and guides others toward goal accomplishments. Encourages cooperative working relationships and cooperation with customer groups. Fosters commitment, team spirit, pride, and trust. Develops leadership in others through mentoring, rewarding, and guiding employees.

3. Results Driven

Accountability—Assures that effective controls are in place to ensure the integrity of the organization. Holds self and others accountable for rules and responsibilities. Can be relied upon to ensure that projects within areas of specific responsibility are completed in a timely manner and within budget. Monitors and evaluates plans; focuses on results and measuring attainment of outcomes.

Customer Service—Balancing interests of a variety of clients; readily readjusts priorities to respond to pressing and changing client demands. Anticipates and meets the need of clients; achieves quality end-products; is committed to continuous improvement of services.

Decisiveness—Exercises good judgment by making sound, well-informed decisions; perceives the implications of decisions; makes effective and timely decisions, even when data is limited or solutions produce unpleasant consequences; is proactive and achievement oriented.

Entrepreneurship—Identifies opportunities to develop and market new products and services within or outside of the organization. Is willing to take risks; initiates actions that involve a deliberate risk to achieve a recognized benefit or advantage.

Problem Solving—Identifies and analyzes problems; distinguishes between relevant and irrelevant information to make logical decisions; provides solutions to individual and organizational problems.

Technical Credibility—Understands and appropriately applies procedures, requirements, regulations, and policies related to specialized expertise. Makes sound hiring and capital resource decisions; addresses training needs. Understands linkages between administrative competencies and mission needs.

4. Business Acumen

Financial Management—Demonstrates broad understanding of principles of financial management and marketing expertise necessary to ensure appropriate funding levels. Prepares, justifies, and/or administers the budget for the program area; uses cost-benefit thinking to set priorities; monitors expenditures in support of programs and policies. Identifies cost-effective approaches. Manages procurement and contracting.

Human Resources Management—Assesses current and future staffing needs based on organizational goals and budget realities. Using merit principles, ensures staff are appropriately selected, developed, utilized, appraised, and rewarded; takes corrective action.

Technology Management—Uses efficient and cost-effective approaches to integrate technology into the workplace and improve program effectiveness. Understands the impact of technological changes on the organization.

5. Building Coalitions/Communications

Influencing/Negotiating—Builds consensus through give and take; persuades others; gains cooperation to obtain information and accomplish goals; facilitates "win-win" situations.

Interpersonal Skills—Considers and responds appropriately to the needs, feelings, and capabilities of different people in different situations; is tactful, compassionate, and sensitive; treats others with respect.

Oral Communication—Makes clear and convincing oral presentations to individuals or groups; listens effectively and clarifies information as needed. Facilitates an open exchange of ideas and fosters an atmosphere of open communication.

Partnering—Develops networks and builds alliances, engages in cross-functional activities; collaborates across boundaries, and finds common ground with a widening range of stakeholders. Utilizes contacts to build and strengthen internal support bases.

Political Savvy—Identifies the internal and external politics that impact the work of the organization. Approaches each problem situation with a clear perception of organizational and political reality; recognizes the impact of alternative courses of action.

Written Communication—Expresses facts and ideas in writing in a clear, convincing, and organized manner.

WHAT IF YOU ARE NOT A NATURAL WRITER?

Suppose you are a dental lab technician or an automotive worker, and you are not used to writing narratives or reports. Suppose you do not like to write? Writing KSA responses is challenging, and it is required.

Look for help. Can you find someone—a family member, a friend, a former supervisor or teacher—who will help you understand what the readers are looking for? Someone who will brainstorm with you to find experiences that showcase your knowledge and skills? Then, after your first or second draft, ask someone who is a careful reader (this may be a different person) to be your "volunteer editor," to read for sense, edit, proofread, and make constructive suggestions.

Refine Your Experiences

Analyze the notes that you have drawn or outlined in Chapter 5. Now is the time to scrutinize these experiences and identify exactly which example or examples best fit your KSA requirement. Regarding this choice, the Human Relations section for the Center for Disease Control (CDC) (www.cdc.gov) offers this advice:

▶ Your examples need to show a **link** between your own experiences and the KSA requirement. Do not assume that the link is obvious to someone else, even though it may be obvious to you. The reviewing panel will not be able to give you credit for experiences that you do not spell out. Remember a few important facts:

▶ It is the **content** of your responses that is rated, not the writing style that you use. It is acceptable to use brief sentences, as long as the reviewers know what you mean.

▶ Very long responses do not guarantee a higher rating than shorter ones. Give the reviewing panel direct and to-the-point responses.

▶ Each KSA requirement may be rated by different readers, but it may not. Repeat information that is crucial and relevant, but try to keep each KSA response fresh.

▶ Remember, do not use abbreviations, acronyms, or jargon, unless it is specific to the job, and then explain them in parentheses. Otherwise, your readers may not understand what you are talking about, and they will not be able to give you credit for your experience.

HELPFUL HINT—FORMAL DOES THE TRICK

When writing your KSA responses, it is better to remain on the side of formality than to risk sounding too casual. Revisit the discussions on tone and word choice in Chapter 6.

Illuminate Your Resume

Do *not* repeat your resume within your KSA response, but *illuminate* important facts or give examples to shed new light on the breadth and scope of your experience. Notice how this resume sample provides an overview of the candidate's experience—in this case, as a trainer for law enforcement officers:

> **Resume:** *Scheduled and conducted training and maintained training records of all law enforcement personnel.*

When writing about her experience, however, the candidate added these details:

> **KSA Response:** *As a supervisor in the training department I conducted sessions on anti-terrorism techniques, security and protection procedures, and suspect-interviewing strategies, to solve this challenge. The results were trained react teams and counterterrorism units.*

This gave the agency fresh information about the experience she could bring to the job. Whatever your education and experience, it deserves to be highlighted in your resume, competencies, and KSA responses. Follow these tips for guidance in presenting your strengths to potential federal employers.

HELPFUL HINT—LEGIBLE IS ESSENTIAL

Illegible handwriting prevents an evaluator from ranking an application. If you cannot use a typewriter or computer to prepare your KSAs, please check that your handwriting is legible.

Showcase Your Role

In fleshing out your notes into full paragraphs, showcase your role in an honest and straightforward manner. The Office of Personnel Management's website at www.usajobs.opm.gov asks these guiding questions to help elicit more detail in your response: Did you work on your own? as part of a team? in a supervisory capacity? as a team leader?

Let the reviewing agency know your role in the projects. For example:

I helped put together conferences. Among my responsibilities were sending invitations, calling potential guests, and preparing the conference materials.

This answer would be stronger if worded this way:

As part of a team of five employees, I helped organize conferences. Among other responsibilities, I coordinated with my coworkers to send invitations, called potential guests, and prepared the conference materials.

Were you promoted while working on a project? If so, mention that too. Note, for example, this response does not mention a promotion:

In my last position, I spent two to three months at a time in the field collecting samples for the study. The following year, I spent most of time in the lab, only going to the field occasionally.

This revision does:

In my position as Project Manager, I spent two to three months at a time in the field, overseeing five specialists who assisted me in collecting samples for the study. The following year, I was promoted to Senior Project Manager, which required that I spend more time in the lab. As a result, I only went to the field occasionally.

Include Timeframes

Timeframes count, so be sure to address these questions: What were the dates or length of time you worked on a project or job? Did you work full-time or part-time? If part-time, what percentage of your time did you do that work? For example, this candidate could have worked in his position for only a few weeks as a part-time employee:

I served as a contractor for the agency. I produced educational videos and safety training sessions.

This response is stronger worded this way:

From 1999–2003, I served as a full-time contractor for the agency. I spent at least 40% of my time producing educational videos and safety training sessions.

If you did not spend substantial time in a particular position, include the dates anyway. Other information, such as the outcome of your experience or the scope and depth of your work will underscore its value.

▶ REVISING AND EDITING

Upon finishing your first draft, your goal is to edit and improve it. Revising and editing are the two last steps of writing that often get left out. **Revising** involves taking a first, or rough, draft and tightening it. You may not need to take each and every one of these steps with every KSA response, but revising can include:

- ▶ improving the organization
- ▶ sharpening the focus
- ▶ clarifying fuzzy logic
- ▶ unifying tone
- ▶ adding details and examples
- ▶ refining the vocabulary
- ▶ eliminating extraneous material or ideas
- ▶ editing for errors in vocabulary, grammar, and usage
- ▶ proofreading for typos and errors in spelling and punctuation

Revisiting Your Draft

Have you ever heard this piece of advice? "Let your draft sit overnight and review it again the next day." This is a valuable piece of advice. It is smart to wait between drafts, if possible. It is also OK to give your KSA response two, three, or even four drafts. At any point, you might engage a friend or colleague (your volunteer editor) to read the draft and make recommendations for changes or for additional information to improve your chances of being rated as "highly qualified."

These general tips may guide you.

- ▶ Be certain you addressed the KSA requirement.
- ▶ Ensure that your examples are readable and interesting.
- ▶ Improve verbs and nouns to accentuate action and results.
- ▶ Add detail to your examples if needed.
- ▶ Proofread your work.

Be Certain You Addressed the KSA Requirement

Have you read and reread the announcement and the KSA requirement? Do you think you have addressed what the agency hiring staff is looking for?

For instance, what does the hiring agency mean by **Ability to Communicate Orally?** Well, they want to know who you communicate with: colleagues? clients? groups? what levels of professionals? Do you negotiate, present, give briefings, handle sensitive situations, mediate solutions, gain consensus? Do you communicate within teams? In your KSA response, your readers want to find experiences demonstrating that you can talk. They also want examples of challenges and goals you have faced that concern speaking. *Have you given them these things?*

Additionally, have you followed special instructions? Did you provide requested copies of licenses, certifications, dates, or other documentation?

Ensure That Your Examples Are Readable and Interesting

Questions to ask yourself and your volunteer editor:

Are my examples easy to understand?

Are my examples interesting?

Are the challenges and the results of my examples clear?

If you or your volunteer editor finds an example is dull or unclear, find out why. Then write another draft, trying to enlighten and clarify the experience.

A Checklist for the Revising Stage

Here are tips to be mindful of during the revision stage:

- ▶ Observe basic writing conventions, such as correct spelling, punctuation, and capitalization (refer to Chapters 6 and 7). Correct errors.
- ▶ Check over sentences and paragraphs to see if they are clear and logical.
- ▶ Check for variety of vocabulary and sentence structure; restructure weak sentences.
- ▶ Focus on specific challenges and results.
- ▶ Include applicable non-federal experience (e.g., leaderships positions, extra-curricular activities, internships, volunteer work, and professional organizations); mention relevant special assignments (e.g., details, task forces, committees).
- ▶ Include relevant awards and commendations.
- ▶ Whenever possible, quantify and qualify (how much, how well, when) your accomplishments (how much/many, how well, when, what scope).
- ▶ Avoid responses that describe your personal beliefs or philosophies.
- ▶ If you have to use abbreviations or acronyms, spell them out the first mention.
- ▶ Proofread the final draft too, to be sure no new mistakes were made in the rewrites.

Improve Verbs and Nouns

The English language is famous for its number of synonyms. When revising your KSA responses, get a hold of a thesaurus and punch up your verbs and nouns a little. You may also revisit Chapter 6 to find suggestions for proactive words.

Engage your reader with interesting words. For example, instead of using the mundane verb *help*, you might use a more compelling verb (according to the sense of your sentence), such as *coach, convince, counsel, galvanize, inspire, invigorate, lobby, persuade, rally, restore, unify, unite*, or *revitalize*.

As for nouns, look for substitutes that have more interest. For instance, in place of the noun *challenge*, which is often overused, you might select *difficulty, dilemma, goal, impediment, issue, obstacle, problem, project*, or *puzzle*. You can review word choice and clarity in Chapter 6.

Add Detail to Your Examples

This is your KSA response mantra: *Quantify and Qualify*. Add details. Be sure you have also considered these factors:

Levels of Supervision. Did you mention groups you have supervised? Did you include working independently with minimum supervision? Were you ever an acting supervisor? Did you also draft memos and reports for your supervisor's signature? Did you manage projects or make decisions in your program areas?

Contacts. In addition to co-workers, clients, and customers, did you mention contact with government officials, headquarters staff, inspectors, or local authorities?

Complexity. Does your example include the size and breadth of projects? That, for example, you maintain LANS/WANS for three locations? Have you mentioned the software you are familiar with? languages you speak? safety standards you follow? certificates, licenses, and accreditation you or your group have earned?

Recognition. Did you consider all relevant awards, commendations, time-off rewards, letters of recognition, newsletter articles?

Trends. Do your examples include the latest vocabulary in your field? (terms or titles such as at-grade, Subject Matter Experts [SMEs], route alignment, Safety Captain, Business Process Engineering [BPE], and so forth)

HELPFUL HINT—RESIST HARD-COPY ADDITIONS

You may be tempted, but, *unless the agency specifically requests it,* resist adding the following items to your package: photocopies of awards, publications, training certificates, letters of recommendation, lengthy job descriptions, writing samples, or photos.

Check Against the Rules in Chapters 6 and 7

After writing your draft of a KSA response, consider and check off Chapter 6 and Chapter 7 rules and guidelines. Some you are probably already good at; some you might want to revisit. Here's a checklist for you:

✓ Use appropriate formality.
✓ Be active, not passive.
✓ Choose a proactive vocabulary.
✓ Understand denotation and connotation.
✓ Convey a positive tone.
✓ Keep it brief and clear.
✓ Understand how the parts of speech work together.
✓ Verify noun/verb agreement.
✓ Correct fragments and run-ons.
✓ Watch verb tense shifts.
✓ Avoid double negatives.
✓ Pay attention to confused and misused words.

✓ Watch your spelling.

✓ Understand punctuation and capitalization rules.

Proofread Your Work

Proofreading means looking for errors in spelling, grammar, punctuation, and typos; it is usually considered part of editing. Using a spell-checking software helps with spelling, but that has drawbacks too. For example, spell checking software may accept the word *form* because it is a valid word, when you meant *from*. This is why proofreading by yourself and your volunteer editor is important. When do you proofread?

Some writers only proofread their work in its final draft. However, you are probably more likely to catch all errors if you proofread *every* draft. But why go to this much trouble?

Misspelled words, grammatical errors, and typos reflect poorly on your application package—and, therefore, on you. *Errors hinder and distract the reader,* distancing him or her from your primary message: "I am the best person for this job."

In summary, remember these four steps in your proofreading process:

1. Use spell-check on your computer.
2. Proofread your writing.
3. Ask a friend or colleague to double-check your work.
4. Proofread the final draft to be sure that no new mistakes were made in revising.

Do not skip these steps because you are in a hurry or because they do not seem all that important to you. They *are* important because, once again, they reflect how much you care about winning this job.

HELPFUL HINT—EDITING AND PROOFREADING STRATEGIES

- Cover your writing with a piece of paper and work your way down, line by line.
- Read your writing aloud or ask someone to read it to you, in order to *hear* mistakes.
- Proofread backward for spelling and spacing errors.
- Use a spellchecker when writing on a PC, but also reread, as spellcheckers miss usage.
- Identify typical errors (for example, problems with subject/verb agreement).
- Look for your own personal, recurring mistakes.
- Get a volunteer editor to read your writing and make constructive comments.

▶ **SUMMARY**

From first draft to final draft, you have learned how to format, write, revise, edit and proofread your KSA responses. Now you need to read sample KSA requirements and responses and to practice these writing techniques over and over. Remember that the most potent KSA responses use the Challenge-Context-Action-Result model, include specific examples of experience, and focus on results.

CHAPTER

9

Sample KSAs and Responses

Learn by example. Or in this case, learn by 24 examples. This final chapter illuminates 24 KSA responses to various KSA requirements, reflecting 24 jobs listings within the six major categories of federal jobs:

1. Student/Internships/Temporary
2. Trades and Labor
3. Professional, Administrative, and Technical Positions
4. Administrative Support Assistant (Clerical)
5. Information Technology and Telecommunications
6. Senior Executive

If you would like, return to Chapter 1 to read more about each of the six categories and the many, many job titles within each category. The following examples are meant to be *representative*. In other words, the KSA requirements for one job will often apply to other or similar jobs; further, the sample KSA responses may be adapted to other jobs and to other knowledge, skills, and abilities.

Now a disclaimer: The examples in this chapter may be *composites* of job listings and/or KSA responses. The experiences are hypothetical, but realistic. Proper names may be real (*Andrews Air Force Base*) or imaginary (*The Lucky Dog pet store*).

It is not recommended that you scan these samples for the exact job you are seeking, or for an exact KSA requirement. As you now know, there are *thousands* of different jobs in the federal government. These samples represent only 24 typical jobs and, for each of those, only one KSA requirement (most jobs have three to six KSA requirements to address). The examples vary in style and format to offer a range of options to fit different job listings. Finally, please do not copy the sample KSA responses—they serve merely as guides, as models. Naturally, your own style should shine through your own experiences and skills.

▶ **STUDENT/INTERN/TEMPORARY**

Human Resources Assistant
KSA: Knowledge of general office automation software, practices, and procedures.

Performed these duties in my present position as Office Assistant at Raintree Employment Agency from 2/1/03 to the present:

- Produced accurate text documents, spreadsheets, databases, and e-mails using these software applications: WordPerfect Office, Microsoft Word, Office Professional, Excel, and Eudora. Often, I took the initiative to teach myself applications with manuals, tutorials, and after-hours practice because there was no one in the office to fill such broad needs. Result: I was entrusted with an interesting variety of duties with increasing responsibility.

- Sorted information in order to fully integrate automation into all aspects of our work, which had not happened yet when I joined Raintree. I coded and entered employee and/or position data into the agency's automated personnel/payroll system. I was trained in maintaining Official Personnel Folders (OPFs). Result: I knew how and where our automated office systems worked and could pass this knowledge on to new recruiters.

- Maintained electronic records and database of employee benefits and employee development programs. Result: I have become proficient in Excel.

- Developed a compelling 42-page PowerPoint presentation for the Raintree Employment Agency owner to use at the 2004 job fair. The presentation received rave reviews, and I was asked to develop a similar presentation for a recruiters' training seminar. Result: I enjoyed creative expression through my expertise with PowerPoint and people became familiar with my computer skills.

- Performed clerical and assistant-level work in support of a staffing and recruitment function, in exact accordance with our city, county, and state's laws, rules, and regulations. Result: I consider myself very familiar with researching and verifying employment regulations.

- Provided online, e-mail, and paper information to applicants, the general public, employees, and supervisors in response to inquiries related to the filling of positions. I recorded questions in Word tables and data in Excel spreadsheets. Result: I practiced several formats in Word tables and Excel spreadsheets.

Volunteer Work: For the past four years, I have used my Word and Excel skills as a volunteer for the Community Council of Idaho Bluffs for approximately six hours a week. I help the webmaster maintain two databases. Further, I sort and print automated contribution letters and envelopes. Contact the ECIB Director, Ms. Marian Weinstein at 800-555-1234.

▶ **STUDENT/INTERN/TEMPORARY**

Census Worker (Bilingual)

KSA: Skill in communication techniques required for professional telephone interviewing and data collection.

While I had the position of telephone interviewer at the Telephone Operations Section, Jeffersonville Telephone Center (JTC)—which has as its function telephone interviewing activities for the National Processing Center (NPC)—I conducted telephone interviews for a wide variety of surveys. From 2001–2003, I functioned independently, dealing with a range of survey complexities in both English and Spanish. When I arrived at the job, however, I challenged myself to learn as much as I could about being a competent and productive interviewer.

At the time, I did not know how to operate a computer terminal, so I requested training at one of JTC's workshops and more extensive training at night school classes (listed below). I finished second in my class out of twenty-two at Framingham Community Center night school. At the annual JTC workshops in 2001–2003, I also enthusiastically filled in gaps in my knowledge by learning about the assigned surveys, better interviewing techniques, and database management. I also learned what to do if the computer system fails.

My primary responsibilities at Jeffersonville Telephone Center required that I master the following skills and abilities:

- telephone respondents on the calling lists, explaining the purpose of the survey or census in both Spanish and English, in order to gain cooperation
- obtain and record the data on a questionnaire or computer
- assure accurate and completed answers to all questions insofar as possible
- make cold calls when asked
- contact previous refusals to persuade the individual to cooperate by providing a thorough explanation of the confidentiality and uses of the survey data
- review information for completeness, edit and assist in clerical processing and/or data entry in both Spanish and English

I have helped resolve special situations and problem cases, including reluctant or irate respondents, and maintaining open lines with the public. Sometimes I was asked to assist a trainee interviewer acquire my skills. This resulted in a cooperative, smoothly-running operation.

My Training Related to This KSA Includes
Jeffersonville Telephone Center Computer Terminal Operations, 2001, 2002, 2003
Framingham Community Center night school, Data Entry and Computer Skills, 2001
Training for volunteer campaign/survey calling to constituents for political campaigns of Rep.
Adam Schuman and Senator Judy Molina, 1998 and 2000

▶ SUPPLEMENTAL QUALIFICATIONS STATEMENTS (SQS)

In some federal job listings with *specialized trades* or *highly technical skills*, in place of KSAs there is a Supplemental Qualifications Statement (SQS) to fill out. Here is one example.

Position Title: MATERIALS ENGINEER

IMPORTANT NOTE: Formatting of tasks contained in this Supplemental Qualifications Statement cannot be altered in any way or for any reason. Attachment sheets or alterations to this task statement are not authorized and will not be used to rank applications.

The responses you provide on the task statement may be verified against the information in your application. Any attempt to exaggerate/conceal/falsify your experience, education, awards, or training can result in removal from employment consideration.

The applicant must complete this information. Please place the number of the most accurate level that applies to your experience, education, and/or training in each task required by this job.

DESCRIPTION OF EXPERIENCE, EDUCATION AND/OR TRAINING LEVELS:

0 I have not had education, training, or experience in performing this task.

1 I have had education or training on this task but have not yet performed it on the job.

2 I have performed this task on the job. A supervisor or senior employee monitored my work on this task to ensure compliance with proper procedures.

3 I have performed this task as a regular part of a job. I have performed it independently and normally without review by a supervisory or senior employee.

4 I have supervised performance of this task or am normally the person who is consulted by other workers to assist them in doing this task because of my expertise.

LEVELS: TASKS:

___ 1. Analyzes materials usage for various component and system designs from a structural integrity point of view.

___ 2. Develops materials qualification requirements for intended applications.

___ 3. Establishes methodologies required for materials specification for developmental programs.

___ 4. Evaluates materials and processes utilized by alternate sources for safety critical parts.

___ 5. Provides materials engineering support in failure analysis of aviation components from service.

___ 6. Performs post-test materials analyses of full-scale component test specimens.

___ 7. Specifies non-destructive inspection methods for field inspection of mechanical components.

___ 8. Provides materials engineering support to fielded systems, evaluates damage, and determines corrective actions.

___ 9. Evaluates materials process-microstructure-properties-performance relationship for a wide range of metallic materials.

___ 10. Presents briefings, technical papers, and reports on materials topics to a technical audience.

___ 11. Presents briefings, and reports to management and other non-materials experts on materials related matters.

___ 12. Prepares and reviews Statements of Work, Airworthiness Qualification Specification, and Plans for Compliance with materials requirements.

▶ TRADES AND LABOR

Fabric Worker
KSA: Ability to do the work of the position without more than normal supervision. (screen out)

In my more than six years of experience as an Army parachute rigger from 1998–2003, and then as a supervisor of parachute riggers and fabric workers from 2003–2004, I demonstrated my strong personal initiative and ability to work with less than normal supervision. As I achieved international recognition in the parachuting field, I earned the following badges and decorations signifying my expertise with all aspects of parachuting.

> Bronze Swiss Parachutist Badge
> Singapore Parachutist Badge
> Australian Army Basic Parachutist Badge
> Military Freefall Parachutist Badge
> Senior Parachutist Badge
> Parachute Rigger Badge
> Parachutist Badge

I am a highly motivated worker, who requires no external motivation to stimulate my strong inclination toward excellence in all endeavors. I am a detail-oriented person. For example, as a safety swimmer during the deliberate parachute water operation, I was commended for being the first person to successfully return every piece of equipment to the base of operations.

In May 2002, we had need of an acting supervisor in our unit of the Army's Parachute School. Subsequently, I was hand picked to supervise eight personnel in the packing, maintenance, and repair of parachutes. In December 2002, I won the respected Army Achievement medal for my "exemplarity performance" as acting supervisor. The medal's accompanying citation read: "Sgt. Nichols is a can-do self-starter. He took charge of an inexperienced crew, identified several deficiencies, and followed through on their improvement. Sgt. Nichols is a consistent top performer, meeting all mission requirements and exceeding all expectations."

SCREEN OUT

When the words "screen out" are printed next to a KSA requirement (as in the Fabric Worker position) that indicates that the KSA is a crucial qualifier for the job opening. If the reviewer feels that your "screen out" response does not demonstrate your strengths in this requirement, you will be screened out—in other words, you will not be considered as a candidate for the position. Therefore, create a blockbuster response: Be sure that the screen-out KSA response you write is articulate, clear, and complete.

▶ TRADES AND LABOR

Cook

KSA: Ability to communicate and direct youth from various ethnic and cultural backgrounds for youth to do quantity cooking and follow oral and written instructions.

The following two experiences demonstrate my proficiency in this KSA:

Job Corps Center, Work Programs Division, Nampa, Idaho, 2001-present

Job Corps is the nation's largest residential education and job training program for at-risk youth, ages 16 through 24. As lead cook in the Job Corps Center's cafeteria, I am responsible for directing two to six student cooks in preparing, cooking, and serving approximately 1,000 healthy meals a day. The job is quite a challenge, especially if one of my student cooks is sick or absent, because the meals still need to be fresh and hot at serving time.

The staff I work with, and the 340 or so residents we serve, are of diverse racial, social, and ethnic backgrounds: Caucasian, African-American, Asian, Native American, and Hispanic. Many of the youth come from violent neighborhoods or broken homes, although they represent social and economic diversity, too. In short, there is much cultural variety in the kitchen and in the cafeteria, which I try to handle in a positive way.

For example, I initiated a cross-cultural tradition at the Center: International lunches are served on Wednesdays. To do this, I direct and guide my cooks in planning and cooking menus (for approximately 340 residents) that represent different cultures. We have had main courses from Thailand, China, Japan, Mexico, Cuba, India, Italy, Germany, Jamaica, France, as well as American specialties like Southwest cuisine, Cajun, and "soul food."

Under my supervision, my student cooks need to be able to read and follow my written directions for inventorying, ordering, storing, cooking, baking, and serving. I encourage them to work together, which results in the ones who do not speak or read English well being helped by the ones who do. On their own initiative, two of my apprentices, Su-Yung and Charlie, decorate the cafeteria with streamers and centerpieces every Wednesday to match the menu.

de Benneville Pines Camp and Conference Center, Angeles Oaks, California, 1998–99.

I served as assistant chef at this mountain-top conference center for 18 months. In this capacity, I was supervised two Latino kitchen helpers with both written and oral instructions. I speak some Spanish, and they spoke some English, so we managed nicely. My challenge of guiding the kitchen helpers to run a kitchen that served from 80–150 campers three meals a day included:

- maintaining the storage areas, food preparation equipment, and cooking equipment
- following sanitation practices in preparing and serving 80–150 meals (cafeteria style)
- preparing box lunches for hikers
- preparing tables for meals and cleaning up after meals
- washing dishes, silver, pots, pans, and glassware
- disposing of galley and mess garbage

- estimating requirements for provisions
- performing laundry duties as directed

I created a bilingual calendar and bulletin board system so Juan, Hector, and I could check off our own duties and cross-check each other's work. My desired effect was achieved: We worked as a well-oiled unit in the kitchen and in the dining hall.

▶ **TRADES AND LABOR**

Hydroelectric Mechanic
KSA: Ability to operate safely.

The three steps in my goal to always operate safely are:

1. **To understand and acknowledge the many dangers inherent in the job.** In my position as Lead Hydroelectric Mechanic at Parker Dam, which is on the California side of the Colorado River, I have learned how challenging and dangerous the job can be. I am fully aware that my work requires frequent climbing, stooping, and working in cramped or awkward positions, on concrete floors and sometimes on very rough and uneven terrain. In addition, it often involves lifting and moving heavy items. Further, we are exposed to grease, oil, solvent fumes, smoke, and dust. We work around water and from great heights, in all kinds of weather and temperatures. We work at all hours and sometimes in double shifts. Being aware of all these elements makes me a better, safer employee.

2. **To practice safety measures at all times.** I am a cautious, detail-oriented person, routinely conscious of safety issues, including wearing appropriate gear and boots, a hard hat, safety goggles, safety mask, and ear phones—each whenever necessary—when overhauling and repairing turbines, generators, pumps, intakes, spillways, and the like. I believe in choosing the right tool and the best tool for each job. I believe following OSHA rules and regulations saves lives.

3. **To teach safety to my crew.** As lead mechanic, I set high safety standards for my crew. I am responsible for daily, on-site safety checks, after which I correct and commend my crew as needed, write reports, and follow-up on changes. For example, during a recent four-hour testing regimen and start-up of rebuilt turbines at Parker Dam, I instructed my fellow mechanics to use special safety precautions, as the area was populated with a construction team and two engineering crews. Last year, we had two new mechanics who arrived nonchalant and lax about safety issues. I decided to solve the problem by inviting a veteran mechanic, who happened to be a wonderful story teller, to join us for coffee and donuts one morning. For a half hour, he told cautionary tales with the underlying theme, "Safety is an everyday commitment." The result was that the whole crew was more alert and respectful of possible dangers.

▶ **TRADES AND LABOR**

Housekeeping Aide

KSA: Knowledge of operating powered equipment (i.e. floor scrubbers, electric floor polishers, vacuum cleaners, and other equipment).

At Ft. Rucker base hospital, I was a Housekeeping Aide for two years, from 2001-03. I was assigned to the Operating Rooms (OR), Critical Care areas, and Emergency Room. I performed a wide variety of tasks which I had to plan carefully in a sequence. I was responsible for keeping my areas in a clean, sanitary, and orderly condition. Consequently, I had to use a vacuum cleaner, a hand-held vacuum, a floor scrubber, and an electric floor polisher in order to complete my duties.

On my own initiative, I either studied manuals or asked for instructions from the Housekeeping Aide Foreman to learn how to operate all the machines. Our foreman, Mr. Silkowski, inspected my assigned areas on a regular basis and always found my work to be "thorough and complete." I was equally responsible for the care and daily maintenance of the tools, materials, and equipment used in the performance of my job.

At Ft. Rucker, the housekeeping staff is not allowed to move equipment or boxes of 50 pounds or more. So sometimes I had to use moving equipment specifically designed for moving items weighing more than 50 pounds. I have other specialized skills that include knowledge of which hospital equipment in the ER and OR can be moved and/or touched during a cleaning operation, as well as knowledge of techniques for cleaning non-conductive floors.

► TRADES AND LABOR

Carpenter
KSA: Knowledge of equipment assembly, construction, repair, etc., of wooden products and structures.

In the past 16 years, I have demonstrated my ability as a carpenter to:

- construct, alter, repair, and maintain wooden structures, such as tool sheds, garages, gazebos, fences, furniture, and bookshelves
- fabricate and repair various wooden products such as shelves, door and window framing, cabinetry, and furniture
- assemble and use hand and powered tools and machines to measure, cut, install, and fasten wooden parts

In 2000–2001, I was commissioned by the Peoria Tribal Cemetery Committee to design and construct five folding deck chairs with Pendleton blanket covers to be given away as the prizes for their fundraising raffle. The resulting raffle proceeds were used to improve the Native American Veterans' monument and grounds, which was very gratifying to me. The Peoria Tribal Newsletter called my chairs "sublimely comfortable."

On past projects, in addition to my own precise work, I have led one to four other carpenters or apprenticing carpenters in the planning, alteration, repair, and maintenance of wooden structures. I have fabricated and repaired wood products such as fine cabinetry, foundry patterns, and form blocks, successfully using power and hand tools. Some jobs have involved arduous and hazardous duties, but I have taken up the challenge to use my tools safely and apply all safety precautions to the worksite. I have made alterations on structural components such as drop ceilings, cabinets, screens, acoustical tile, doors, windows, and all trim. I have repaired or replaced studs, mud sills, girders, steps, porches, hand rails, and floors including parquet, asphalt, linoleum, and hardwood. I have approached other challenges such as repairing roof rafters and sheathing and performing minor roofing duties. My supervisors have praised me for consistently producing sound, useful, attractive wood products in a safe work environment.

Volunteer Work
When my time coincided with their work needs, I have volunteered for the last eight years with Habitat for Humanity helping build safe, comfortable housing alongside members of low-income families. When needed, I trained up to twelve volunteers at a time on construction and woodworking, including framing, cabinets, stairs, windows, trim, and so forth.

▶ **TRADES AND LABOR**

Laborer

KSA: Ability to follow instructions and to interpret written instructions from supervisor, manufacturer's literature, specifications, etc. (other than blueprints).

My latest experience as a laborer was in 2002–03, while I was working at the Ulysses S. Grant National Historic Site, Maintenance Division, in St. Louis, Missouri. The site has five historic structures (main house, stone building, barn, chicken house, and ice house). The area consists of 9.65 acres. I followed a duty sheet each day I worked, reading and interpreting instructions for the day. I read and followed instruction and maintenance manuals for all our equipment. The duties that I had to understand clearly to perform well included:

- mowing lawns with walk-behind power mowers and riding mowers
- raking leaves and pulling weeds
- trimming shrubs and edging walkways using hand-held power equipment
- performing snow and ice removal by shoveling snow, chopping ice, and sanding walkways
- hauling material, supplies, and equipment to and from job site areas using self-powered equipment or hand trucks
- performing custodial duties, cleaning park offices, and workshop areas
- performing laborer duties in support of skilled trades people in carpentry, masonry, painting, and roofing
- operating power equipment such as chainsaw, jack hammer, ax, picks, and tampers

I know I performed these tasks carefully and according to instructions because I received five average quarterly performance reviews and two raises within 17 months.

▶ PROFESSIONAL, ADMINISTRATIVE, AND TECHNICAL POSITIONS

Program Director

KSA: Ability to plan, organize, and manage projects.

In 1997–2002, I served as one of Oklahoma's domestic service program managers in Tulsa. In March of 1998, following the notification that the federal agency Volunteers in Service to America (VISTA) would receive a dramatically reduced budget locally, I recognized that two important programs would be discontinued, including vital nutrition education and well-baby programs for several local communities.

As a state program developer, I took the initiative to outline and discuss the situation with other state project managers and project proposal writers. I convinced a local VISTA program director and a county budget committee member to travel with me to Oklahoma City to discuss our proposal of state funding with legislators. I traveled to Arkansas to evaluate similar nutrition education projects and well-baby clinics on several occasions, meeting with counterparts to learn what I could. I adapted a few of their ideas to work better in our state. I negotiated directly with Oklahoma lawmakers and their clerks on program definitions and funding. I prepared a briefing booklet for state representatives including the data on projected numbers of eligible newborns, children, and adults in their communities, if these programs were to expand into other districts.

Results: I achieved a comprehensive, cooperative agreement with the state for commitments of $650,000 a year. Additionally, I brought in three other state agencies to assist with providing services and additional funding and support.

▶ PROFESSIONAL, ADMINISTRATIVE, AND TECHNICAL POSITIONS

Correctional Officer

KSA: Ability to make decisions and act quickly, particularly under stress.

For three years I have worked for the City of Detroit as a probation officer. I specialize in counseling juvenile offenders and juvenile recidivists. I try to keep them from returning to jail or prison by guiding them to find support networks. I also help them find jobs, housing, substance-abuse rehabilitation, and mentors. I have to make decisions rapidly, and under stress.

Re-arresting one of my parolees. When a witness called the Detroit Police Department to report that one of my parolees had a gun on his person, I had to accompany the two arresting police officers. We were armed and wearing flak vests. As odd as it may sound, the Department policy is that I was to lead the officers to James's apartment and make the arrest. When we arrived, however, we discovered James had his five-year-old daughter with him in the apartment—I could hear her talking from our position in the hallway. I remembered he had a daughter named Maggie. James sounded manic, but not hostile. However, we felt we had a potential hostage situation.

While the police officers were ready to radio for a SWAT team, I motioned for them to wait. It was very tense, but I remained calm and I was confident I could help. I thought about what form of psychology would work best with James. I put my jacket on over my vest and gun, so he would not feel threatened. I knocked on the door and announced myself. James recognized me and let me in, sounding scared, but not confrontational. Remembering how much James had talked about his daughter at our appointments and how he had missed her while in prison, I was able to persuade him not to do anything to hurt her future or his chances of leniency. He gave himself up, handed me his gun, and we carried Maggie to her aunt's apartment down the hall. I was very proud of myself for how the situation was handled.

Other Experience Pertinent to This KSA

Big Brother, 1990–95

Volunteer Youth Counselor at Main Street Mission, 1995–98

Shan Tung Kung Fu Association, black belt

Red Cross Emergency Training Certification

Community Emergency Leader Training

▶ **PROFESSIONAL, ADMINISTRATIVE, AND TECHNICAL POSITIONS**

Clinical Nurse (RN)

KSA: Ability to be flexible within schedules and duties, such as overtime work, shift work and/or rotating shifts.

As a charge nurse, I perform a variety of administrative and floor duties as an extension and in support of the head nurse. I need to be very flexible if I am going to ask others to be flexible. I make nursing care assignments to various skill levels of professional and nonprofessional personnel, while I myself accept various assignments. I am willing to substitute for other nurses or participate in rotating shifts when necessary.

During my first position as RN, in a Health and Human Services Clinic in Cooper, Michigan, I learned to adjust to overtime work, shift work, and rotating shift work. This flexibility is absolutely necessary to ensure peace among the staff and to provide coverage on evenings, weekends, holidays, and in other special situations, such as the widespread flu outbreak we had in the winter of 1999.

During that experience, my assistant was on maternity leave when two dozen patients contracted the flu. I was responsible for providing a full range of nursing services that extended beyond caring for the sick; it included assessing, diagnosing, and evaluating the medical condition of our patients. I worked many overtime hours to help our health care team restore our patients' health.

▶ PROFESSIONAL, ADMINISTRATIVE, AND TECHNICAL POSITIONS

Procurement Technician
KSA: Ability to plan and organize work, and set priorities.

For five years, I have been working on a public mass transit project in the San Luis Valley, which is partially funded by the Federal Transportation Administration. In the early stages of project planning, the community through which the light-rail train was going to run grew concerned over landscaping and irrigation issues. Subsequently, I was asked to support ten public "town hall" meetings with only two weeks' preparation time.

- I attended meetings or teleconferenced with project management staff, community relations, and elected officials to understand their needs and meet their priorities.
- I researched and procured meeting sites that could hold 200 people. Those sites had to be handicapped accessible and have their own parking facilities.
- I planned the procurement, on a competitive basis, of catering for hors d'oeuvres and drinks; graphics services for posters and banners; signage for meetings; and reproduction services for flyers, handouts, badges, and name tents.
- I coordinated the renting/borrowing and transportation of extras such as projection equipment for electronic presentations and podiums and sound systems for the speakers and the attendees.
- For two meetings, I procured, on a competitive basis, a Mandarin translator, which my agency does not regularly employ.

I reprioritized my duties when, in the final days of preparation, I had to add two additional meetings. Another complication occurred when Councilperson Hamm requested a shuttle be made available to elderly attendees for four meetings in his district that were near assisted-living homes.

Because of quickly evolving details regarding these meetings, I not only had to set weekly and daily priorities, but re-examine them hourly. As a consequence of my excellent organizing skills, the dozen meetings ran smoothly and the community turned out for the event. I received a commendation from the Project Manager that read in part: "Superior support on an outreach effort crucial to this project." I also received a complimentary letter from Councilperson Hamm, thanking me for enabling his elderly constituency to attend the meetings.

▶ PROFESSIONAL, ADMINISTRATIVE, AND TECHNICAL POSITIONS

Botanist

KSA: Ability to work as part of a team.

I have had the experience of working as part of a team for 4 1/2 years in my current job at the Plant Sciences Institute Systematic Botany and Mycology Laboratory, in Beltsville, Maryland. In this position, I assist two other scientists in the review of scientific names of vascular plants and their characteristics, and in making the results available through the Internet. The three of us alternate our tasks so as not to get too bored or entrenched in one job.

In some cases, one botanist assists another, as when Dr. Culpepper searches scientific literature and web resources for taxonomic information on nomenclature, classification, common names, geographical distribution, and economic uses of vascular plants. I take over then, searching the International Code of Botanical Nomenclature to evaluate these scientific names. Dr. Lewis-Smith is not as proficient at Internet research, so he often enters the data we have collected at the Germplasm Resources Information Network (GRIN) taxonomy area. We take turns continually monitoring taxonomic data for currency and consistency, correcting errors, and standardizing data where necessary. Quarterly, Dr. Lewis-Smith and I alternate responsibility for the management of our botanical literature resources, including the reprints, books, and journals used in our research.

In this way, we work well as a team, complementing each other, and yet enjoying some degree of variety in our research work.

▶ PROFESSIONAL, ADMINISTRATIVE, AND TECHNICAL POSITIONS

Management Analyst
KSA: Ability to communicate in writing.

In my consulting position with Castle Associates, I do a large amount of writing to help solve management challenges. I write technical and administrative memos and study reports, which identify actual and potential problem areas in interrelated work processes, the underlying source of operating difficulties, trends, significant management accomplishments, merit/deficiency situations, and areas of imbalance. These papers always include recommendations for improvement in the studied areas. Examples of the kinds of clear and directed studies I produce are as follows:

- As a management analyst, I write **memos** that represent the Castle Associates Regional Office (RO) position on proposed procedures and work processes. This involves evaluating the affect of alternative actions on the work processes under consideration, and how best to use manpower and resources and the identification of other alternatives worthy of consideration. My challenge is to consolidate information and comments from multiple components into one memo representing the RO position on a given issue. An example of this type of product is the formulation of office comments on the design of the new National Fishery Control System users' comments. A committee reviewed the release to evaluate if all valuable work processes were included and to identify (possibly) more efficient design alternatives. In most cases, I consolidated the comments of the committee and formulated the final office comment memo for our client. The consequence was a satisfied client who made adjustments in management techniques.

- I have been involved in Castle Associates' **periodic reports** on national TS/incubation workloads since 1982. These reports were researched and written by me and a team of two to four analysts. The final product was most often consolidated from other area reports and the consolidated annual report was issued to the Secretary of Labor. The result met our work goals and the charge of the Department of Labor to "prepare the American people for new and better jobs."

- I also wrote **position papers** detailing the Castle Associates' position on administrative, workload processing, or work measurement issues. An example of this type of product is a memo prepared for Central Office in July 1999 stating the RO's position on the issue of productivity measurement in the field stations. This memo presents our views on the Groening-Reed Productivity Analysis Project: It pointed out in detail what we considered to be flaws in their basic assumptions. It then listed the specific major problems that should be addressed to provide valid productivity measures for all the field stations. The RO's proposals concerning the elements necessary for an acceptable productivity measure were presented. I was proud that this position paper resulted in an eventual 65% increase in productivity within two years of its release.

In addition, I have completed nine semester hours of writing courses at Columbia University in New York City. At Columbia, I was a member of the student newspaper staff for two years. Since January 2002, I have served as the Corresponding Secretary for the Sigma Kappa National Sorority.

▶ ADMINISTRATIVE SUPPORT ASSISTANT (CLERICAL)

Staff Assistant
KSA: Knowledge of office procedures and practices.

In 2002 and 2003, as Staff Assistant to Jane Gibout, Esq., of the law firm of Gray, Sainati, and Pomplun, I undertook a variety of short- and long-term projects for Ms. Gibout. These projects entailed all of these office procedures and practices:

    dictation
    keyboarding legal documents
    composing letters
    processing and logging correspondence
    e-mailing and archiving e-mails
    mail merging, mailings
    filing
    database management
    online and records research
    summarizing and reporting to my supervisor
    filing legal documents with the court
    managing Ms. Gibout's schedule

For seven months, I assisted on a case of alleged bankruptcy fraud. This included reviewing and logging related correspondence and writing notifications to the defendants on the progress of the case. I interacted with our private investigator, our clients, and court personnel on the telephone and in person. I also conducted Internet and County Records searches for real estate and other assets. I managed all office functions for this one fraud case, keeping logs and records of all documents.

Before working for Ms. Gibout as a staff assistant, I worked for over two years (1999–2001) as a legal secretary for Gia Vincent, Esq., a patent attorney in Atlanta. After working in two legal office environments, I have had considerable opportunity to hone my office and writing skills.

Job-related Skills, Awards, and Training
    Working knowledge of Microsoft Word, Office, Excel, Monzilla, and EsqWare
    Typing speed = 65 wpm
    Fluent in German and French
    High Performance Award, 2002
    Acting Treasurer, Atlanta Legal Secretary Association, 2002
    Member, Atlanta Legal Secretary Association, 1999–present
    Legal Secretary Certificate, Armstrong Secretarial Institute (top honors), 1999

▶ ADMINISTRATIVE SUPPORT ASSISTANT (CLERICAL)

Clerk Stenographer and Assistant
KSA: Knowledge of grammar, spelling, capitalization, and punctuation.

In my current position as Junior Office Manager of The Lucky Dog pet store chain (2000–2004), I work essentially without supervision and, therefore, must rely on my own extensive knowledge of grammar, spelling, capitalization, and punctuation. I often type correspondence, e-mails, and memoranda in final form for all three stores. In addition, I take dictation from two supervisors, transcribe and type it, and occasionally transcribe Dictaphone dictation as well. The challenge is to complete all of my daily duties and still feel I have done exacting work in everything I write, from lists to memoranda.

I am a detail-oriented person, and I enjoy proofreading and editing my own work. This has led others to ask my advice with grammar and usage issues in their own business letters and reports. I have been told by colleagues, distributors, and clients alike that my correspondence is clear and succinct and that it displays a professional look. I believe this reflects well both on me and on the company.

In my previous position as Receptionist, then Assistant, to the Director of National Education Center (1996–2000), I first developed proficiency in grammar, spelling, and punctuation by taking nights courses at an adult business school. I recognized that I needed to polish these skills in order to handle a variety of complex office management duties. I eventually became known to the staff for my excellent spelling, grammar, capitalization, and punctuation skills, which were sought out by my colleagues.

Education and Training Related to This KSA

Basic Office Management Workshop, PDA Associates, 2 days, 2002

Business English course, NEC, 16 weeks, 1997

English Grammar course, NEC, 8 weeks, 1997

Clerk-Typist course, NEC, 8 weeks, 1996

Stenography course, NEC, 16 weeks, 1996

▶ ADMINISTRATIVE SUPPORT ASSISTANT (CLERICAL)

Office Automation Assistant
KSA: Ability to communicate orally.

While working as a receptionist and office assistant, I have discovered that I have considerable oral communication skills. For example, my duties at the Purple Circus Candy Company include handling routine telephone inquiries for information about our company, job opportunities, and factory tours.

I enjoy answering questions on the telephone, as well as face-to-face, and I guarantee complete, friendly answers, or I promise to research what the customer needs and get back to him or her. People tell me I have a "smile in my voice." I am naturally enthusiastic and able to convey my thoughts well verbally, but I believe a vital part of being a truly effective communicator is to be a thoughtful listener. And sometimes that means you have to "listen between the lines."

For example, one experience I had recently was when a customer called to inquire about our factory/warehouse tours, which we offer every Friday morning, from 8:00 A.M. to 9:45 A.M., and again from 10:00 A.M. to noon. These tours include an introductory video about the history and products of Purple Circus, a guided tour of the factory, a visit to the warehouse and loading docks, and the presentation of gift bags to our guests on the tour. This caller was the organizer of field trips for an "umbrella school" for homeschoolers. She had 45–50 homeschooling kids and their parents who had voted unanimously to tour our candy plant. I gave her a rundown on our Friday touring hours. She hesitated and said, "OK, well then, I am sorry, I guess we won't be able to do it." I heard the disappointment in her voice. I prevailed upon her to stay on the line and tell me why they could not make it. Apparently, the majority of kids in this group had three-hour science labs in physical science and biology on Friday mornings. Their designated field trip days were Wednesday or Saturday. I told her not to worry, I would find a solution.

The next morning I went to speak with Erin, the woman who directs the tours, and I persuaded her to offer a special Wednesday tour to the homeschooling group. I convinced her that these homeschoolers would make a very lively tour group and that "Forty-five to fifty *future loyal customers* would be very impressed by a big, busy company that cared enough to adjust *our* schedule to *their* schedule." My persuasive speech worked and the tour was arranged. As a favor to Erin, I suggested I would communicate with the factory foreman and the warehouse manager to notify them of the special Wednesday tour. They were very accommodating (and grateful I had thought to inform them).

I have also successfully instructed new employees on the workings of our telephones, PCs, printers, FAX machine, and scanner. I think I have a very good method of give-and-take in my oral communications.

▶ ADMINISTRATIVE SUPPORT ASSISTANT (CLERICAL)

Personal Assistant
KSA: Ability to write non-technical correspondence.

At Cheng Lee Enterprises, I am the only administrative assistant in my unit. I handle the writing of responses for most non-technical correspondence received and for all administrative matters within the unit. I also compose in-house e-mails for my supervisors. I have written business letters for my supervisors and for the company director. I respond using various form letters that we have on file. Sometimes I have to draft a letter from start to finish depending on what the inquiry is about.

For example, an employee may need a statement regarding leave balances, which I would write. Or I might have to produce a memo to the warehouse regarding supply shortages. When Mr. Senn, the production manager, writes memos, he will give them to me in draft form, and I will rewrite them to ensure proper grammar and to put them into the right format. I have to use my judgment in deciding which form letter or template is most appropriate.

Awards

    Cheng Lee Enterprises Employee of the Month, June 2001 and February 2003

    Golden Mouse Word Processing Medal, 2002

    Top 10% of class at National Secretarial Academy, 1999

Education and Training Related to This KSA

    National Secretarial Academy, Business English and Administrative Assistant courses, Secretarial Certification, 1998–99

    Aurora City College, AA Degree, English, 1998

▶ INFORMATION TECHNOLOGY AND TELECOMMUNICATIONS

Telecommunications Specialist
KSA: Skill in providing professional and courteous customer service to users in person and/or via the telephone.

It seems that IT and Telecommunications Specialists have the reputation of being aloof or even nasty when it comes to providing customer service, particularly within their own companies or agencies. I try to disprove that stereotype. I believe I support customers in a friendly and professional manner.

I am currently working as a Telecommunications Specialist for the Internal Revenue Service in Lanham, Ohio. My job has many duties, but a very important one is satisfying the questions and problems of intra-agency telecommunications users. My charge is to ensure efficient continued operations and customer support of various voice and data communications systems. I help to monitor these systems, and when called in, I identify and resolve day-to-day performance or capacity problems.

I always try to leave my own worries behind when I handle either in-person or telephone customer service calls, because I identify with their frustrations and their desire for immediate solutions. For my tech support work, I am exceedingly proud to have earned two merit awards from my department for "professional and exemplary customer service, above and beyond the call of duty."

I also provide technical and policy guidance to management, and here is where customer service can be a complex challenge. On occasion, I recommend network design plans that include new software requirements or equipment needs (for example, to address ever-growing security concerns). This usually means presenting information relevant to taking the steps necessary to get the budget people to find the funds for this expenditure. However, I tell my supervisors that my recommendations are really a form of customer service to the agency. It is my duty to politely-but-firmly support whatever changes and expenditures I sincerely believe will advance this agency's telecommunications capabilities and its security.

▶ INFORMATION TECHNOLOGY AND TELECOMMUNICATIONS

Computer Scientist
KSA: Knowledge of conceptual design of computer systems.

I have always had a passion for computers and computer systems. As a dilligent graduate student at Stanford University in the Computer Science Department, I demonstrated my ability to conduct operational analysis and to formulate system concept architectural designs, software development, functional specifications, system integration, and documentation aspects of computer systems. I was fortunate to learn from and work with engineers, scientists, and senior academics on language processors and computer operating systems, and to determine the status of many performance, reliability, and quality characteristics of computer systems.

As a University of Virginia undergraduate, I learned about computer organization and assembly-language programming, mastering a good amount of material on the internal components of individual computers. At both the graduate and undergraduate levels, I studied the conceptual design of distributed and parallel computer systems.

I gained strong experience in inspecting, repairing, and maintaining computers and systems as a paid Computer Technician for the French Department at University of Virginia. I performed troubleshooting to the component level. I implemented diagnostic programs and used testing equipment. I learned how to inspect and repair hardware such as keyboards, terminals, line printers, display stations, tape drives, card readers, multiplexes, and so forth.

Education and Training Related to This KSA

Master of Science degree, Computer Science, Stanford University (2002)

Bachelor of Science degree, Computer Science, University of Virginia, graduated Summa Cum Laude (1999)

▶ INFORMATION TECHNOLOGY AND TELECOMMUNICATIONS

Information Technology Instructor
KSA: Knowledge of principles, methods, and techniques of instruction.

As Information Technology Instructor at the Information Management Training Division, School of Applied Information Technology, Foreign Service Institute, in Washington, DC, I practiced a range of instruction methods. I provided Information Technology (IT) training to officers and staff of the Foreign Service and Civil Service throughout the State Department. This training covered file management, commercial off-the-shelf software (or "COTS," e.g., Windows), and custom applications developed by and/or for the State Department. I employed various effective methods of instruction:

Personal Experience. During the first class meeting, I began by asking each student to share briefly a little bit about his or her job. I guided students to elaborate on software and IT issues in their jobs. This way, during instruction, I was able to use personal examples from each person's work day.

Lecture and Q & A. I led 15 IT workshops for all position levels on the importance of maintaining department files, including file nomenclature, folder hierarchy, and backing up information. Everyone in the State Department and Foreign Service was required to attend certain IT classes, which meant my learners encompassed all levels of computer knowledge, department responsibility, and job longevity. This broad spectrum required that I cover all types of IT situations. I lectured and also held Question and Answer sessions, where we would share our IT knowledge.

Expert Speakers. Since September 11, 2001, the IT Security Measures Program was given highest priority by the U.S. Department of Homeland Security and the State Department. There was some resistance in my first classes regarding maintaining files in a secure manner. With this challenge, I complemented my own instruction with speakers from the Department of Homeland Security and the FBI, who narrated excellent first-hand experiences of security loss and risk. I also worked hard to show that each person who touched agency data was an important link in our security program.

Metaphors and Graphics. Another of my goals was to eliminate eccentric file naming and storage techniques, so that others in an agency or intra-agency might have easy access (when allowed) to each person's data. I did this through frequent metaphors (citing classic examples of a hard disk as a file cabinet with hundreds of drawers or a pie that could be cut into hundreds of slices). When appropriate, PowerPoint presentations, screen captures, and other graphics were used in teaching software and IT principles, especially for the visual learners among my students.

Hands-on Learning. I believe that no pedagogical technique works as well when teaching IT as hands-on practice and step-throughs. Each of my classes was broken into groups of no more than five to allow for plenty of hands-on exercises and drills, which I monitored. Then we reconvened to discuss problems and solutions.

Peer Teaching. When assigning computer project assignments or software exercises, I ask my students to pair off or work in small groups of three. I encourage them to include, if possible, one member who knows the software or who is a quick study in IT. Peer teaching (with the instructor as a resource) can work very well for two reasons: Peers may have similar stumbling blocks and the one who is teaching is also discovering what he/she does not fully grasp and reinforcing what he/she does.

Training and Certification Pertinent to This KSA

  Microsoft Certified Systems Engineer (MCSE) for Windows 2000 Certification

  Microsoft Certified Trainer (MCT) Certification

  Comptia A+ and Network+ Certification

  Fluency in Microsoft Office

  Workshops in Technical Course Instruction and Curriculum Design

▶ INFORMATION TECHNOLOGY AND TELECOMMUNICATIONS

Systems Analyst

KSA: Ability to interpret and follow oral instructions.

Throughout my academic career, I was required to listen to lectures and direction in large lecture halls, as well as in small, intimate classrooms. In college I was a French minor, so my very small language classes necessitated following oral instructions to the letter (and in French), or be asked to leave. Studying a spoken foreign language is an excellent way to master following directions.

In all courses, I followed oral instructions in order to do the correct research, or submit a complete project. Sometimes I had to figure out what the instructor really meant or ask questions if it just was not clear. In these cases, discussing the instructions with a fellow student or the Teaching Assistant was all it took to clarify them.

My eccentric Shakespeare professor, Dr. Williams, would sometimes dictate cryptic assignments with page and line numbers, which would lead us to words and lines within Shakespeare passages that we had to interpret in order to understand the assignment.

I enrolled in a night school cooking class a few years ago. Our instructor, the head chef at a local trendy bistro, gave all cooking instructions orally. We were not to take notes, except for listing recipe ingredients, and he rarely entertained questions. In that course, I truly learned how to listen well, how to use mnemonic devices (memory tricks), and how to watch others as they also interpreted our chef-teacher.

Early in my career as a systems analyst, I learned how important it is to be able to follow through on my assignments, even when instructions were not detailed, not specific enough, or were confusing. I learned to use common sense and logic to interpret. I learned to seek out a mentor's advice when necessary. Many years of staff and project management meetings have enhanced my listening skills, while teaching me to cull the essential information.

In my current position, I provide leadership for all aspects of project management and day-to-day coordination with technical staff, so *I* need to try to give the clearest, most definitive instructions I can. Project management, which includes overseeing technical projects within a team of eight to twenty members, requires strong interpersonal skills and the ability to effectively listen and speak.

Education and Training Related to This KSA

Knowledge of tools and management software: HP GlancePlus, HP OpenView, HP PerfView, Omni-back, HP-UX shell scripting

Advanced management-level training with American Airlines, 2000

Bachelor of Science degree, Computer Science, University of California Santa Cruz, 1998

▶ **SENIOR EXECUTIVE**

Senior Equal Opportunity Advisor

KSA: Knowledge of the concepts, principles, and methods of equal opportunity or of fair housing; knowledge of equal opportunity laws being enforced.

- Completed 3 1/2 years of specialized experience in operational and lead responsibility as Equal Opportunity (EO) advisor in the Housing and Urban Development (HUD) district office in New Orleans, working under the senior EO Officer, Dr. Delores Sanchez.
- Served as principal EO advisor to the district's HUD Program Center Director on all matters related to equal opportunity in housing and facilities, economic opportunity, civil rights, and non-discrimination in all implementation of programs of HUD in the geographic area of Louisiana and Mississippi.
- Supervised and trained six EO advisors and EO assistants from 2001–2003, including detailing equal opportunity law.
- Was responsible for overseeing the fair housing enforcement, compliance, and operational functions and responsibilities in connection with equal opportunity and civil rights, including those under the Fair Housing Act, Title VI of the Civil Rights Act of 1964, Section 109 of the Housing and Community Development Act of 1974, as amended, Section 504 of the Rehabilitation Act of 1973, the Americans with Disabilities Act, the Age Discrimination Act of 1975, and relevant Executive Orders in Louisiana and Mississippi.
- Demonstrated the highest level of ability in these duties, resulting in a HUD Commendation and the 2003 EO Advisor of the Year Award.

In 1999 I was a Fair Housing Investigator for the State of Georgia. I mastered these requirements:

- making personal contacts, within state, county, city and university governing bodies
- investigating and analyzing problems in EO and fair housing areas
- facilitating meetings with fair housing attorneys and paralegals and their clients
- preparing well-written, high-quality analytical investigation reports which clearly support conclusions and decisions

▶ **SENIOR EXECUTIVE**

Postal Supervisor

KSA: Ability to forecast mail volume and human resource needs.

The two experiences described below indicate my ability to predict future mail volume and workforce requirements.

In 2002, while assigned to the La Crescenta Remote Encoding Center (REC), I was monitoring the Crestview plant status reports. Fortunately, I noticed that we had a very low volume of images to process. I knew that the plant's volume projections indicated a high volume of mail to be processed and identified the need for a maximum number of keyers to be working at our consoles. I informed the Crestview plant of the problem and diplomatically directed them to turn off the Recognition Coprocessor Reader (RCR). This, I knew, would permit a quicker transfer of images. Results: My judgment and actions enabled the staff to process all the images and meet the Crestview plant's clearance time. The appropriate number of keyers fit the projected volume of mail.

During my detail as acting supervisor at the Pasadena REC, I received a request for more keyers for the La Crescenta plant. Their staff needed to compensate for the arrival of late mail yet to be processed by the Input Sub-System (ISS) and they had two employees who were out sick. I consulted with the Pasadena plant and, due to their low volume of mail, I was able to shift more keyers to La Crescenta. **Results:** The increase in keyers to the La Crescenta plant allowed us to process all of the mail in a timely manner; by working cooperatively, we were able to complete our tasks and have the satisfaction of meeting goal under a stressful situation.

▶ **SUMMARY**

Remember, the examples in this chapter are meant to be *representative*. These samples represent only 24 typical jobs and, for each of those, only one KSA requirement. It will not be helpful to copy the sample KSA responses—they serve merely as guides. Now it is your turn to find a job, write winning KSAs, and get a great federal job. Good luck!